Listening to Young Children

The Mosaic approach

Alison Clark and Peter Moss

Second edition

NCB's vision is a society in which all children and young people are valued and their rights are respected.

By advancing the well-being of all children and young people across every aspect of their lives, NCB aims to:

- reduce inequalities in childhood
- ensure children and young people have a strong voice in all matters that affect their lives
- promote positive images of children and young people
- enhance the health and well-being of all children and young people
- encourage positive and supportive family, and other environments.

NCB has adopted and works within the UN Convention on the Rights of the Child.

Published by NCB

NCB, 8 Wakley Street, London EC1V 7QE
Tel: 0207 843 6000
Website: www.ncb.org.uk
Registered charity number: 258825

NCB works in partnership with Children in Scotland (www.childreninscotland.org.uk) and Children in Wales (www.childreninwales.org.uk).

ISBN: 978 1 907969 26 3

The Joseph Rowntree Foundation has supported the original project as part of its programme of research and innovative development projects, which it hopes will be of value to policy makers and practitioners.

British Library Cataloguing in Publication Data

A catalogue record for this book is available from the British Library

Typeset by Saxon Graphics Ltd, Derby
Printed in the UK by Cambrian Printers Ltd, Aberystwyth.
Printed on paper from certified forests using vegetable based inks, chemical free plates and presses running alcohol free.

FSC
Mixed Sources
Product group from well-managed forests and other controlled sources

Cert no. TT-COC-2200
www.fsc.org
© 1996 Forest Stewardship Council

Contents

Foreword to the second edition

Early years researchers, teachers and students will welcome the second edition of *Listening to Young Children*. The earlier book has been very influential in informing ethical research methods with young children, and many of us have found the Mosaic approach very useful as we plan and implement research in the early years. In this edition, the first part of the title has been highlighted: the value of *listening*, not for knowledge 'extraction' but for knowledge creation. In this edition the 'listening' agenda, retaining its connection with research, has been given a bit more weight, emphasising the link between listening and action or what we might call *formative* listening, a parallel with the idea of *formative* assessment. It's about listening that makes a difference.

The introduction to Part 1 comments that 'At the time of writing the first edition of this book it was unusual to see young children's perspectives of their early childhood institutions accepted as a necessary part of exploring the quality of provision'. And, as the authors comment, children's perspectives are not just a necessary part of *exploring* the quality of provision, they are integral to the quality of provision itself. The challenges and pitfalls of listening to children are raised clearly in this edition, and with this in mind, it nicely accompanies the valuable 2005 book edited by Alison Clark, Anne Trine Kjørholt and Peter Moss entitled *Beyond Listening*. This book broadens the scope of the first edition. It emphasises that children have the right not only to have their voices heard in matters that concern them, especially when they are the subjects of research, but also that listening is central to responsive and reciprocal relationships when the object is teaching and learning. After all, teachers are researchers too: seeking the children's perspectives, noticing recognising and documenting their interests and achievements. In my view, the book nicely blurs the boundaries between the two endeavours: research and pedagogy.

Multimodal possibilities have developed considerably over the last ten years, and the mosaic agenda of this book, the range of modes of communication, has also been extended by the addition of more recent examples, the inclusion of ideas for seeking the perspectives of non-verbal babies and children, and the new opportunities for children to take the initiative that the 21st century digital technology. Of course, the ethical principles of agency, accessibility and authenticity when researching with young children remain the same no matter what the mode of communication or representation, and these principles, the backbone of the first edition remain the key message here too.

As in the earlier book, an enjoyment of, and a commitment to seeking, the views of young people, reflected so well in Vivian Gussin Paley's work, is an underlying theme. Listening to others is central to recognising and coordinating multiple perspectives, a skill and disposition for the making of meaning in new contexts. This, in my view, is an important purpose for education in the broadest sense. Another theme here is democracy in the classroom – or the childcare centre, nursery, kindergarten, playcentre, play group, preschool or kōhanga reo (a New Zealand Māori immersion early childhood setting) – establishing and sustaining 'a cultural climate which values children's opinions'. The final purpose here is, for me, to inform research and pedagogy that aims for the democratic engagement of all participants. It looks forward to early years educational sites as places where people listen to each other and co-construct meanings together. I am sure that this book will contribute to that vision for education in the early years.

Margaret Carr
Hamilton, New Zealand
July 2011

Preface to the second edition

Since this book was first published in 2001 there has been continued policy and practice interest in the UK and internationally in ways of gathering the perspectives of young children. This has been matched by researchers' interests in finding methods which may enable young children's perspectives to be made more visible. The first edition of this book marked a particular interest in exploratory ways of listening to young children's perspectives through research. This builds on the work of earlier advocates. Among those who found time to combine working with young children and writing were Vivian Gussin Paley in the USA (for example 1981; 1997) and Judy Miller in England (Miller, 1997). In Vivian Gussin Paley's work we see rich examples of the competences of young children carefully documented by an adult who started from the premise that there was always more to learn from children. Judy Miller's work has been as an advocate for listening to young children providing practical starting points for new ways of supporting young children's agency.

Reaction to the Mosaic approach over the past decade, and to this volume in particular suggests that this slim account provides a way in to thinking about research with young children, repositioning young children within the research process whilst drawing on a long tradition of early childhood practice and democracy in education. It can be seen in parallel with movements in compulsory education about pupil voice.

The research study outlined here is based on the first of three empirical studies undertaken by myself with Peter Moss to listen to young children's perspectives of their early childhood institutions. The subsequent research has built on this initial study to involve young children, practitioners and parents in physical changes to early childhood environments, in outdoor spaces (Clark and Moss, 2005) and in the design and review of learning environments (Clark, 2010a). Other researchers, based in the UK and internationally, have taken up and adapted the approach in their own studies, for example Johanna Einarsdottir in Iceland and Alison Stephenson in New Zealand.

The continued development of the Mosaic approach has been born out of cross-national, cross-disciplinary and cross-generational dialogue. The edited book, *Beyond listening* (Clark, Moss and Kjørholt, 2005) was the result of such discussions. Two parallel networks have fostered this development. The first is an international research network formed by myself and Deborah Harcourt (Australian Catholic University) in 2004 following the 14th European Early Education Research Association conference. This Special Interest Group on Children's Perspectives in Research has provided a sounding board for theoretical, methodological and ethical discussions about listening to young children. The second network has been the Listening to Young Children Network, part of the valuable work of the Early Childhood Unit at the National Children's Bureau. This network, supported by the advisory group to which I belong, has sought to demonstrate how young children's perspectives can play an integral part in establishing a 'listening culture' within early childhood institutions where adults and children both receive and contribute. These discussions have been enriched by my encounters with early childhood students and practitioners through the Institute of Education, Roehampton University and the Open University.

These twin stimuli of both research and practice have continued to challenge my ways of applying and talking and writing about the Mosaic approach over the past ten years. This second edition presents an opportunity to step back and to re-examine this initial study whilst providing new readers with some pointers as to how this work has been adapted by myself and others. New short introductions have been added to each of the three parts of this book. The main body of the text which relates to the research study has not been changed. Part 3 has been updated to include examples of how the Mosaic approach has been adapted by practitioners. My hope is that this research study remains relevant as a marker in the development of this field of work and as a possible way in for those seeking a different way of tuning in to young children. The conversations continue.

Alison Clark
London, May 2011

Acknowledgements

First edition

Firstly, thank you to the children, parents and practitioners at Thomas Coram Early Childhood Centre and Field Lane Homeless Families Centre, for the generosity of their time and for their insights.

We gratefully acknowledge the financial support of the Joseph Rowntree Foundation throughout this project and the advice and encouragement of Susan Taylor, Senior Research Manager at the Foundation, who oversaw the project.

This project has been a joint undertaking between the Thomas Coram Research Unit and Coram Family. This research would not have been possible without the vision and collaboration of Gillian Pugh, Chief Executive of Coram Family.

The Joseph Rowntree Foundation convened an Advisory Group for this study, who provided valuable advice, suggestions and support. Members of the Advisory Group were: Gillian Pugh, Coram Family; Maggie Bishop, Coram Family; Margy Whalley, Pen Green Centre; Lesley Whitney, Camden LEA; Tricia Cresswell, Newcastle and North Tyneside Health Authority; Teresa Smith, University of Oxford; Iram Siraj-Blatchford, Institutive of Education, University of London; Lonica Vanclay, Family Welfare Association and Keith Morris, DfEE.

We would also like to thank the academics and practitioners who Alison Clark met on her study tour to Denmark and Norway, including Jens Qvortrup; Jan Kampmann; Ole Langsted; Jytte Juul Jensen; Jens Esberg; Lisa Hammershoj Jensen; Tone Kronkvist; Ellen Os; Anne Trine Kjørholt; Grethe Ringnes; Sissel Ostberg; Gunver Løkken; Erik Sigsgaard; Søren Smidt; Anne-Lise Holmvik; staff of the Children's Council in Copenhagen, and Tove Hauge, special advisor to the Ombudsman for Children, Oslo; also friends, Bob and Sheila Smith. Special thanks for the welcome received at the early childhood institutions in the Stjordal kommune, Norway and in Århus, Denmark.

This research has benefited from dialogue with many other individuals including Priscilla Alderson; Nicky Road; Tina Hyder and Margaret Carr.

Second edition

We would like to thank the following individuals for being able to include examples of adaptations of the Mosaic approach: Petra Morden, Vicky Fowkes, Chris Malone, Sarah Birch, Alida Savedra, Jo Bearpark, Terri Task, Caroline Adams, Stella Mitchell; Alice Paige-Smith and Jonathan Rix. Special acknowledgement to Lucy Williams, Project Manager of the Young Children's Voices Network for her significant contribution to supporting listening to young children.

If we are constantly astonished at the child's perceptiveness, It means that we do not take them seriously.

Janusz Korczak (Joseph, 1999)

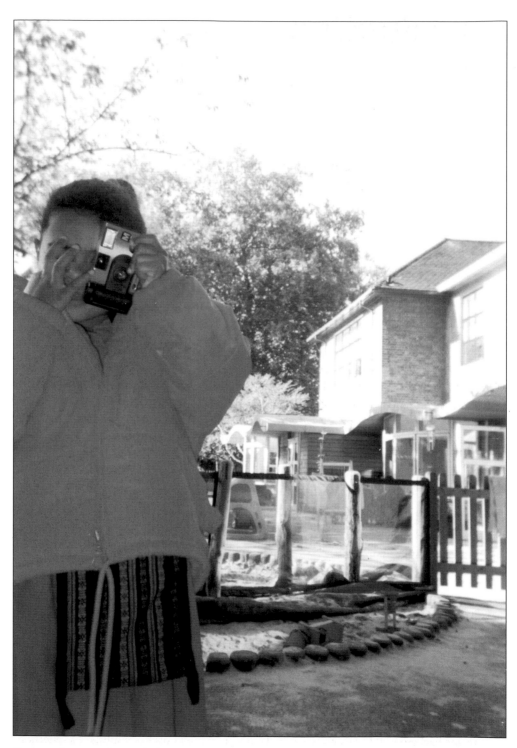

Cameras in action: Meryl photographed by Clare (age 4)

Introduction

Although it is becoming more common to talk about including children's perspectives in reviews of services, the rhetoric outpaces practice (McNeish, 1999). This is particularly the case for young children. Traditional methods of consultation with user groups require imaginative rethinking if the views and experiences of young children are to be listened to and responded to by adults. This report outlines a new framework: the Mosaic approach for listening to young children's perspectives on their daily lives. The Mosaic approach is a way of listening that acknowledges children and adults as co-constructors of meaning. It is an integrated approach which combines the visual with the verbal.

An important influence in developing this approach has been methods used in participatory appraisal (PA). These methods, also referred to as 'participatory rural appraisal' or 'participatory learning in action' have their origins in rural development work. Participatory appraisal is about empowering poor communities to have a 'voice' in changes within their own communities. A range of imaginative methodologies are used which do not rely on the written word. But participatory appraisal is as much about the process of dialogue, reflection and action as it is about the tools used (O'Kane, 2000).

Second, the Mosaic approach has been inspired by 'pedagogical documentation' as developed in the pre-schools of Reggio Emilia in Northern Italy.[1]

---

1   Since writing the first edition, two books have been published by key contributors to the early childhood programme of Reggio Emilia. The former director of the municipal education centres, Carlina Rinaldi has published 'In Dialogue with Reggio Emila: listening, researching and learning (2006). Vea Vecchi, one of the first artelieristas (educators with an arts background) to be appointed in the Reggio pre-schools has published a reflection on her work: 'Art and creativity in Reggio Emilia: exploring the role and potential of ateliers in early childhood education' (2009).

The project

The Mosaic approach has been developed with three and four year olds in an early childhood institution and has been adapted to work with children under two, children for whom English is an additional language, practitioners and parents.

The aim has been to find practical ways to contribute to the development of services that are responsive to the 'voice of the child' and which recognise young children's competencies. This study has also paid close attention to the relation between theory, concept and practice.

This study has been exploratory in nature. Areas for further development have emerged during the eighteen months of the study and will be the focus of future work. The study has been part of a wider two year project to describe and evaluate a multiagency network or 'campus model' of service provision (Wigfall and Moss, 2001) based at Coram Community Campus, in the King's Cross area of London. The Coram Community Campus (CCC) is an innovative model of service provision for children and families. It brings together onto one site a range of services which offer care, education, support and other facilities for young children and their families living in a deprived and multi-ethnic area of Inner London. The services are provided by a number of agencies, public and private, with one agency, the Coram Family[2] (formerly the Thomas Coram Foundation, a long established children's charity) providing the site as well as coordination between services and agencies. This study reflects work with children from one of the two nurseries on the site, the Thomas Coram Early Childhood Centre (TCECC) funded by Camden Council which together with the Parents' Centre was awarded Early Excellence Centre status by the DfEE in 1999. Children from Field Lane Homeless Families Centre, one of the two homelessness projects on the Campus, have also been involved in the study.

The original intention was to focus on children under eight years of age. Following observations carried out in different services on the Campus, an extensive literature review and a study tour to Scandinavia, it was decided to concentrate on children under five years. This is the area where the complexities of listening to young children are highlighted. The main focus of the study has been two key groups within the TCECC: children age three to four years in the kindergarten and children under two in the nursery. Pilot work has

---

2   The children's charity now uses the working name Coram

also been carried out with refugee children attending Field Lane, the homeless families project. While the majority of children using this service are under five, two older refugee children age six and nine were also involved in this stage of the project. The possibility of working with children with disabilities who used the service, KIDs, was investigated. However, at the time of conducting the fieldwork, KIDs had only recently relocated to the Campus and it did not prove possible to include this service in the study. Twenty children in total have been involved in this study, together with six practitioners, three from each setting, and five parents.

The report

This report details the progress to date on developing the Mosaic approach to listening to young children. It has been compiled by Alison Clark, researcher on the project with Peter Moss, project leader. The Mosaic approach enables young children and adults to be involved in 'meaning making' together. This is a multi-method approach in which children's own photographs, tours and maps can be joined to talking and observing to gain deeper understanding of children's lives.

The Mosaic approach also has potential as a tool to use with older children, particularly those with communication difficulties or for whom English is an additional language.

Part 1 of the report describes the framework for listening we have adopted. Part 2 details the development of the Mosaic approach during this study, including the direct work with young children, parents and practitioners. Part 3 explores the practicalities, pitfalls and potential for developing this framework in early childhood institutions.

Part 1
Framework for listening

Part 1 explains the framework adopted for listening to young children in the Mosaic approach. This is an epistemological approach, that is to say it contains particular views about the nature of knowledge, how it can be constructed and communicated.

Knowledge creation rather than knowledge extraction

This emphasis on facilitating the process of knowledge production has become increasingly important in the way research studies using the Mosaic approach have developed (Clark, 2010a and 2010b).

> *Participatory methods are those that facilitate the process of knowledge production as opposed to knowledge 'gathering', as is the case with methods such as individual interviews, surveys and checklists.*
>
> (Veale, 2005: 254)

This is not about research encounters as a chance to extract one 'truth' but as opportunities for creating meanings. An environment is created in which research participants whether young children or adults are given the opportunity to step back and to reflect on their views and experiences. A range of research methods are brought together that are designed to play to the strengths of the research participants. The purpose is to facilitate the co-construction of meanings.

Knowledge that challenges dominant discourses about whose knowledge counts

The Mosaic approach is participatory research and as such challenges the dominant discourses about whose knowledge counts. At the time of writing the first edition of this book it was unusual to see young children's perspectives of their early childhood institutions accepted as a necessary part of exploring the quality of provision.

There have been theoretical and methodological barriers in the way of making such practice more common. This has required articulating *why* it is important to value young children's views and experiences and *how* it is possible to do so. There is a parallel here with other earlier debates about whose knowledge counts. Feminist researchers have made the case for both why it is necessary for women's everyday experiences to be listened to and how these accounts should be represented (for example (Ribbens and Edwards,1998; Oakley, 2000).

Disabled children, young people and adults have also faced prejudice and other barriers to having their own expertise recognised. Reidun Tangen, a Norwegian researcher draws a parallel between debates around 'listening to young children's voices' and theoretical and methodological approaches to gathering the views and experiences of children with special educational needs (2008). The challenge here is not trying to speak for the 'other' but to provide a context in which the experiences of individuals from seldom heard groups are given status (see Pascal and Bertram, 2009).

Knowledge constructed using different modes of communication

The individual tools or methods in the Mosaic approach were chosen to enable young children to explore their experiences of being in an early childhood institution through talking, walking, making and reviewing. These forms of expression were chosen to be closely aligned to how young children might choose to communicate with friends and family. These informal modes of communication might be different from the formal more literacy-based forms of communication dominant in early childhood settings in the UK. A range of methods and modes was necessary in order to draw on the strengths of individual children and to offer a range of opportunities to think. A multi-method approach offers several opportunities as Alison Stephenson, a New Zealand researcher comments:

> As Clark and Moss (2001) had found with the 'Mosaic approach', using a range of strategies was effective because not only did it allow for triangulation of data, but it meant that children could select the activity they preferred and so, to use their image, for each child a quite different mosaic pattern might be created.
>
> (Stephenson, 2009: 136)

The purpose however of opening up different modes of communication is not to necessarily to reach a single neat answer as 'triangulation' might suggest but to reveal the complexities of lived experience. Richardson and Adams St. Pierre (2008) describes this process as crystallisation rather than triangulation, a process of looking at the world that is multi-dimensional.

Developing the Mosaic approach

In subsequent studies we have built on this epistemological framework by making more explicit the views about young children which underpinned the development of the Mosaic approach. This is an acknowledgement of how implicit views about childhood influence the way adults interact with young children whether as researchers, practitioners or parents:

> Young children as 'experts in their own lives'
>
> Young children as skilful communicators
>
> Young children as rights holders
>
> Young children as meaning makers
>
> (Clark and Moss, 2005: 5)

These principles have become shorthand for the framework described in Part 1 of this book. Each of these principles are explained in more detail elsewhere (Clark and Moss, 2005: 5–8 and see Appendix).

The framework for listening

We have sought a framework for listening to young children which is:

- *multi-method:* recognises the different 'voices' or languages of children
- *participatory:* treats children as experts and agents in their own lives
- *reflexive:* includes children, practitioners and parents in reflecting on meanings; addresses the question of interpretation
- *adaptable:* can be applied in a variety of early childhood institutions
- *focused on children's lived experiences:* can be used for a variety of purposes including looking at lives lived rather than only at knowledge gained or care received
- *embedded into practice:* a framework for listening which has the potential to be both used as an evaluative tool and to become embedded into early years practice.

Multi-method approach

It is important to understand listening to be a process which is not limited to the spoken word. The phrase 'voice of the child' may suggest the transmission of ideas only through words, but listening to young children, including pre-verbal children, needs to be a process which is open to the many creative ways young children use to express their views and experiences. Malaguzzi's phrase 'the hundred languages of children' (Edwards and others, 1998) reminds us of this potential.

The voices of young children begin at birth (Pugh and Selleck, 1996) and children can 'speak' to adults through their play, their actions and reactions (Goldschmied and Jackson, 1994). There is a current interest in different disciplines and professions to find new ways to communicate with young children (see for example, Pugh and Selleck, 1996; Miller, 1997).[1] This has informed our decision to look for a multi-method approach.

---

1   See for example the training and resources produced by Lancaster and Kirby on behalf of Coram (2010) *Listening to young children.* 2nd edition, that have made a significant contribution to promoting ways of listening to and communicating with young children.

We have chosen a framework for listening which is an integrated approach, combining the 'visual' with the 'verbal'. The value of *talking* to young children about their daily lives is not overlooked. However, tools are suggested which also enable young children to communicate their ideas and feelings to adults in other symbolic ways, for example through photographs or drawing. These methods may in turn serve as a springboard for more talking, listening and reflecting.

The Mosaic approach is therefore a multi-method process. A range of different techniques has been placed together to gain young children's views and experiences of their lives in a particular early childhood institution. Some of these methods are those traditionally used to inform adults about young children's lives, whilst others offer new opportunities for 'listening on all channels' (Marchant, 1999).

Participatory process

Our aim has been to find an approach which begins from the starting point of 'children as experts in their own lives' (Langsted, 1994). We believe children, like adults, are 'social actors' who are 'beings' rather than 'becomings' (Qvortrup, 1987).[2] This is in keeping with the approach taken in the new discipline of Childhood Studies, in which children's ideas, approaches to life, choices and relationships are viewed as of interest in their own right (James and Prout, 1997). Recognising children's competencies can help adults reflect on the limitations of their understanding of children's lives; to listen to children more rather than assume we already know the answers. This has been the starting point for our framework for listening.

We have adapted participatory techniques as developed in participatory appraisal, for use with young children. Originally these participatory methods were created to enable non-literate adults in the Majority World to play an active part in decision-making at a local level. Techniques include the use of mapping and modelling, drawing and collage, child to child interviewing and drama and puppetry. Johnson and Ivan-Smith describe the use of such tools

---

2   Lee (2001) and Prout (2005) have been among those to emphasise the importance of seeing children and adults as both beings and becomings. This enables respect for children in the present at the same time as recognising children and adults are involved in complex processes of change: '...both children and adults should be seen through a multiplicity of becomings in which all are incomplete and dependent' (Prout, 2005: 67).

with children as enabling adults to 'view the world through the lens of children and young people' (Johnson and others, 1998). It is not only a question of seeing the world from children's perspectives but of acknowledging their rights to express their point of view or to remain silent. We are keen that a participatory approach to listening is respectful of children's views and also of their silences.

Reflexive

We want to emphasise that listening is an active process, involving not just hearing but interpreting, constructing meaning and responding. Children and adults are part of this process. Carlina Rinaldi, former head of the pre-school services in Reggio Emilia speaks of 'a pedagogy of listening': 'the most important verb is to listen, to hear and to be open to others, to listen with all our senses' (Rinaldi, 1999).[3] Listening as a process involves interpretation. It is an 'active emotion' involving the listener in making meaning in an interpretive process. The Mosaic approach can provide a tangible focus for those responsible for young children to reflect together on children's perspectives, led by the children themselves.

The reflexive approach we have chosen to adopt has much in common with the idea of pedagogical documentation used in the nurseries of Reggio Emilia. Listening, observing, gathering documentation and interpretation are key elements.

Documentation is about communication (Dahlberg, Moss and Pence, 1999: 154). It is a framework for laying out in the open ideas, perceptions and attitudes held by young children and adults in a way that promotes lively exchange and increased understanding: interpretation is acknowledged as an essential part of documentation. The range of perspectives may lead to different interpretations. However, this is not viewed as a weakness but as a way to further 'communication, reflection and action' (Dahlberg, Moss and Pence, 1999: 158). Children are not left on the outside of these discussions but are central to these exchanges about meaning. They are co-constructors (James and Prout, 1997).

---

3   The pedagogy listening: this concept has been explored further by Rinaldi in Clark, Moss and Kjørholt (eds) (2005) volume about children's perspectives of early childhood services. This is followed by a chapter looking at the process of listening using the Mosaic approach in relation to pedagogy of listening (Clark, 2005). See Appendix Further reading about the Mosaic approach.

Practitioners and parents are co-constructors too, but are freed from the need to know all the answers.

We take the concept of documentation a step further by introducing a range of participatory tools so young children have more opportunity to share their perspectives.

Adaptable

We set out in our research to develop a framework for listening which could be adapted to work in different early childhood institutions. This approach is less about particular methods than a way of conceptualising 'listening' and the relationships and processes involved. The important factors to remember are to find methods which begin from the starting point of children as experts in their own lives and which open up as many different ways of communicating this competency as possible. Some techniques may be more appropriate according to the gender mix of a group or the different cultures of the children. Other possibilities may relate to particular skills of practitioners working with the children. In the Coram Community Campus study we used a range of visual and verbal methods adapted to fit the particular early childhood institution.

Focused on children's lived experiences

We have also sought an approach which can be used for a variety of purposes including looking at 'lives lived' rather than focusing only on knowledge gained or care received. We emphasise the importance of exploring children's views and experiences of *everyday life* in the institutions they attend; as members of communities rather than consumers or users of a product. Viewing children as consumers may lead to a shallow understanding of children's satisfaction rather than deepening our understanding of the complexities of their everyday lives. References to young children as 'consumers' of services has grown in recent years. Economic changes which gathered force in the 1980s emphasised the rights of consumers to express their views about the services they received. The language of the market place entered social policy. In the field of education in England this led to the Parent's

Charter (Department of Education and Science, 1991). Here, parents and not children were seen as the users of the education system. There has been a movement in the 1990s to treat children themselves as 'consumers'. This can be seen in the way marketing companies are increasingly interested in listening to children's views, including those of young children.[4]

The gathering of 'consumer' or 'customer' views is part of a wider discussion about quality. Early childhood institutions have become the focus for research, measures, standards and good practice guidelines about quality. This drive for accountability and effectiveness in public services continued during the 1990s. Few attempts have been made to gather pre-school children's perspectives on their childcare environment (Armstrong and Sugawara, 1989; Berghout Austin and others, 1996).[5] The Childcare Audits are one of the most recent policy expressions of the desire to include user views in the improvement of services. One of the challenges posed by these audits is how to communicate young children's views.

Much of the expertise in listening to young children has been concerned with children as learners. Early childhood educators are involved in this day to day task. We need to look further however, not only at the process of learning but the framework within which educators are operating. Within the 'learning frame' there is a wide range of approaches or pedagogies which view children in different ways. Some see young children as empty vessels waiting to be filled with knowledge. Within this frame children are the objects into which learning is poured. Other approaches see children as active participants in their own learning. Listening to young children is a key element in approaches to learning which view children as active participants. Paley (1986: 125) describes how listening to children in her classroom provided a new way of relating to children: 'The rules of teaching had now changed; I now wanted to hear the answers I could not myself invent.'

---

4   The marketing interest in children including young children as consumers has continued to increase. One contributing factor has been the advance in digital interactive technologies that present new contexts in which children are consumers (see for example, Calvert, 2008).

5   There has been a burgeoning of initiatives to include young children's perspectives in the evaluation of early childhood provision, supported by policy changes and legislation. An important change since the publication of the first edition has been the Childcare Act 2006. Section 3 of this Act places a duty on local authorities in England to take into account young children's views of the services they receive.

Two Early Childhood Education (ECE) approaches which are explicit about viewing children as competent 'beings not becomings' are the Reggio Emilia approach, as discussed above and Te Whaariki, the New Zealand early years curriculum. Te Whaariki is a child-centred curriculum, which starts from children's learning dispositions and attitudes, rather than prescribed curriculum areas. The five strands of the curriculum are: belonging, well-being, exploration, communication and contribution. Empowerment runs as a theme throughout Te Whaariki. This approach has inspired a curriculum framework in the UK, developed by the Early Childhood Education Forum: Quality and Diversity (Early Childhood Education Forum, 1998). 'Participating and contributing' is one of the key areas of this framework. There has been a concerted effort by early years practitioners to maintain this child-centred approach within the Foundation Stage of the National Curriculum.[6]

Embedded into practice

We have been concerned to develop an approach to listening to young children which has the potential to be both used as an evaluative tool and to become embedded into early years practice.

Our intention is to broaden the approach of regarding listening as consultancy: 'what do you think about this?', to seeing listening as an ongoing conversation. Listening then becomes embedded in relationships based on 'an ethics of encounter' (Dahlberg, Moss and Pence, 1999: 156). Children are respected as is difference; so we are not trying to seek 'the voice of *the* child', nor trying to make children's voices echo adult voices, nor requiring consensus.

---

6   The Early Years Foundation Stage, statutory framework came into force in England in September 2008 and is concerned with the learning, development and care of children from birth up until the age of six. Listening to young children and parents is one of the key features which underpin the child-centred themes and principles.

Part 2
The Mosaic approach

Part 2 describes the different methods brought together in this first study to form the Mosaic approach. We originally identified two stages:

- Stage 1: children and adults gathering documentation.
- Stage 2: piecing together information for dialogue, reflection and interpretation.

We subsequently added a third stage to the Mosaic approach:

- Stage 3: deciding on continuity and change.

This stage was added to make explicit the intended link between listening and action. This emphasises the applied nature of this approach to research with participants and is keeping with adopting a participatory paradigm. Dialogue, reflection and interpretation have remained key features of working in this way but we have highlighted the relationship between listening and change. This acts as a reminder of listening being more than a tick-box activity to meet policy objectives. We have pursued these reflections on 'beyond listening' with academics and researchers (Clark, Moss and Kjørholt, 2005).

Part 2 describes each individual method in detail with examples of some of the new understandings gained from the young children involved. Case studies are given of three children to illustrate how the themes emerging from using the different methods were brought together. However, the specific methods are not intended as a finite list but as a way of conceptualising 'listening' and focusing on the relationships that are involved (see page 10).

Participatory visual methods have played an important part in developing the Mosaic approach as the use of the visual in this way fits with the desire to challenge the research relationships between an adult researcher and a young participant. Prosser and Loxley (2008) describes participant-generated visual material as one category of visual methods. This has become an increasingly popular method in qualitative research in education and the social sciences (for example see Thomson, 2008). One of the possibilities raised by these methods is the increased status that may be given to perspectives that are shared in a visual way. A child of three, for example may struggle to convey the importance of a particular space or person within their early childhood institution but taking a photograph or making a map with their chosen images may provide a stronger 'voice'. However, as we will return to in Part 3, no set of methods provide 'magic answers'. Incorporating the visual in research highlights the need for interpretation whatever the age group we are working with:

> It is worth emphasising that there is no single or 'correct' answer to the question, 'What does this image mean?' or 'What is this ad saying?' Since there is no law which can guarantee that things will have 'one true meaning', or that meanings won't change over time, work in this area is bound to be interpretative ...
>
> (Hall, 1997: 9)[1]

The research context and research questions will continue to be key in deciding what research methodology and methods to adopt. Participatory visual methods will not be appropriate in every research context or answer every research question. However, if research questions focus on gathering the perspectives of 'insider views' (Tangen, 2008) then this raft of methods may provide powerful tools if handled with care.

---

[1]   Stuart Hall cited in Rose, G. (2007) *Visual methodologies: an introduction to the interpretation of visual methods.* 2nd edition. London: Sage, xiv.

Stage 1
Children and adults gathering documentation

Pieces of the mosaic

Observation is the first of these pieces or tools. Listening also involves watching. Slowing down enough to watch how children spend their time in an early childhood institution is a necessary beginning, even for those who work in that environment.

Child conferencing is the second of these more traditional pieces of the mosaic. This is a short interview schedule similar to the format developed by the Centre for Language in Primary Education in the 1980s. We adapted our child conferencing questions from the schedule devised by Bernadette Duffy, Head of Thomas Coram Early Childhood Centre.

We have joined the perspectives provided by observation and child conferencing with innovative participatory methods for young children: the use of *cameras*, *tours* and *mapping*. We have been seeking tools that play to the strengths of young children, methods that are active, accessible and not reliant on the written or spoken word. This combination of techniques provides the scope for flexibility and creativity.

This rich combination of data is drawn together in the Mosaic approach to form a 'living picture' of what being in this place is like for these children. This provides a new platform for listening.

Observation

We have used the question, 'Do you listen to me?' as the basis for our observations with children under five in both TCECC and Field Lane. This question has been adapted from the questions used in the evaluative framework for the New Zealand early years programme, Te Whaariki.

We have also adapted the use of narrative accounts or 'Nursery Stories' devised by Elfer and Selleck during their three year study of under threes in day care (Elfer and Selleck, 1999).

How can observation contribute to the Mosaic approach? Observation, based around the two questions of 'what is it like to be here?' and 'do you listen to me?' provides one way of making children's lives more visible. The narrative accounts of individual episodes can be fed into discussions with children, parents, practitioners and researchers to ask 'what is happening here?' The following is an example taken from observation of a key group of three and four year olds playing together.

Observation in action: three and four year olds

Gaby said she liked to play best. This was the impression I gained from having observed Gaby's key group. She was often involved with a group of friends in organising complicated imaginative play. One session took place in the afternoon by the computer table on a very wet day in June. It was a game of hospitals and houses in which Gaby was one of the major players. She had a baby (a doll) who wasn't well. She lay the doll on the mouse mat for the computer and used the 'mouse' to pump the baby's chest and make her better: 'Daddy is coming home soon. The baby is OK. She is moving.' More children joined in. There were eight children involved in this game at one point. Two of the boys were told to be babies too. Gaby's baby was Gary and Meryl's baby was John. 'Let me change your nappy darling,' said Gaby to Gary.

Researcher's field notes

This 'snapshot' provides a record of play in progress which can be discussed with children, practitioners and parents as an example of time spent in the nursery. This particular example highlighted the importance of role play to Gaby's enjoyment of being in the nursery. This was confirmed by later conversations with her keyworker and mother[2] (see Case Study 3: Gaby page 45).

---

2   Keyworker – at the time of conducting this study this was the term given in this centre to the early childhood practitioner who was the named individual with special responsibility for the children in their group. Following the introduction of the Early Years Foundation Stage this role has been identified as a key person role: 'the named member of staff with whom a child has more contact than other adults. This adult shows a special interest in the child through close personal interaction day to day. The key person can help the young child to deal with separation anxiety' (Glossary, EYFS 2008).

What did the use of observation reveal about children's lives lived in the nursery?

The researcher's accounts included the following themes:

Children's games

Meal times

Interaction with peers and with adults

Use of outside space

Use of inside space, including corridors

The observations of pre-verbal children were of particular importance. All-day observations of children under two provided the opportunity to 'listen' to their body language; their different cries, facial expressions, noises and movements to build up an impression of what being in the nursery was like for these very young children (see Case Study 1: Toni page 38).

Observation in action: pre-verbal children

At ten o'clock in the morning Alan is sitting on a large mat playing with a set of bells. Alan picks up one of the large shiny tins and looks at his reflection in the tin. Tim is playing with bricks and an improvised toy slide, posting bricks down the tube. 'Oo' he says in delight as the brick disappears and appears again. He then wanders and finds a whisk (actual metal kitchen whisk) and bashes it against the ground and enjoying the noise.

Robin comes over and gives me a musical toy when I sit down and then goes back to watching Tim.

Alan hears a noise and crawls over to a baby gym which has chains and bells and Chinese bells attached. He claps and looks round to smile. He stays playing, totally absorbed.

Alan is giggling with the chains which hang from the baby gym. He hits them and they make a jangling noise. If he hits the ground underneath it moves the chains too.

Bobby (keyworker) comes over to watch Alan. 'Alan, you are being busy.' Alan stops playing. 'I'm sorry, did I interrupt you.'

Researcher's field notes

The child in this account, Alan, had special needs and at almost two was not talking or walking. Observation helped to establish his enjoyment of music and the affection that was shared between Alan and his keyworker.

In searching for new ways of listening to young children it is important we do not abandon established practices such as observation which can contribute to our understanding of children's lives. However, this form of observation only gives an adult perspective on children's lives. This piece of the mosaic needs to be seen in conjunction with other sources of information, especially those based on participatory methods.

Child conferencing

Talking to young children is an important part of the Mosaic approach. Child conferencing provides one formal structure for talking to young children about their institution. We have adapted this style of interviewing into a more active child-focused process.

A small number of studies have attempted to include young children's views in evaluations. These have included the use of interviews (Hennessy, 1999) and role play as the basis for interviewing young children (Evans and Fuller, 1996).

Child conferencing was already in use in TCECC as a tool to involve children's views in the internal audit process. The short interview schedule has 14 questions based around key themes of why children come to nursery, the role of adults, favourite activities and people and worst people and activities. The interview ends with an open-ended question to provide the opportunity for children to add any further information they think is important. Some children choose to add a drawing at this point or to sign their name.

We carried out the child conferencing with a group of seven children in the kindergarten of TCECC in July 1999 and repeated it with those children who were still a member in November 1999. This provided opportunities for the children to reflect on their previous responses and to assess how their situations and feelings had changed.

Child conferencing in action Clare (four years) interviewed in July and November 1999

- *Why do you come to nursery?*

  July

  I like playing with the children and my Mummy has to take me to nursery and she has to work and so does my Dad and he has to get up very early.

  November

  Sometimes (he has to get up very early).

- *What do you like best?*

  July

  Making masks ... and you pop the balloon and after that you put paper on and you paint masks.

  November

  No comments added.

- *What don't you like about being here?*

  July

  L is very silly.

  November

  L is on holiday now.

- *Who are your favourite people?*

  July

  N, M, B, S and K (*practitioners*)

  November

  No comments added.

- *Who don't you like?*

  July

  Chimpanzees!

  November

  No comments added.

- *What do grown-ups do at nursery?*

  July

  They play with me.

  November

  Do some drawing with me.

- **What should grown-ups do at nursery?**

  July
  They should go on their lunch break and do their work.

  November
  No comments added.

- **Where is your favourite place in the nursery?**

  July
  Outside and inside and having fruit time.

  November
  No comments added.

- **Which part of the nursery don't you like?**

  July
  The staffroom, 'cos they have their lunch break.

  November
  No comments added.

- **What do you find difficult?**

  July
  No comment.

  November
  Writing.

- **What is the food like?**

  July
  I like potatoes.

  November
  No comments added.

- **What has been your best day in Bob's group?**

  July
  Going to the station.

  November
  I painted in the winter an aeroplane of my Mum and Dad and me. We were going to Spain.

Excerpt from Child conferencing

What did child conferencing reveal about children's perspectives?

Favourite people: friends and keyworkers.

Role of adults: to play with children, to keep order.

People children didn't like: individual children; boys.

Favourite places: outside spaces, 'key group' room.

Places children didn't like: the staff room; 'the building with the blinds down'.

Difficult things: another child's behaviour; footpath on the way to nursery.

Favourite activities: making masks; imaginative play; the slide.

Best day in the nursery: days out, playing hide and seek, playing with Lego.

People

Two girls mentioned adults as their favourite people. Clare named five adults as her favourite people in the nursery (see transcript above). Five children named other children. One of the girls later took many photos of the favourite people she named. Three children named specific children they didn't like. Clare made a diversionary response to the question of who she didn't like: 'chimpanzees'. We were sitting next to a book trolley with a book about chimpanzees in view. This stresses the importance of recording the context in which child conferencing takes place as well as individual responses.

Places

Outside places were mentioned most frequently. One child expressed an equal preference for inside and outside places. Another child's favourite place seemed to be connected to where his mother knew he would be: 'I live in here (Gold room) so my Mummy knows where I am. I like playing with sharks.'

The children's answers to which places they didn't like were very individual. Clare named the staffroom as one place she didn't like. This was a space where children did not generally go. It seems understandable that a child who liked adult company would not be keen on the room where adults went to be with other adults.

Gary mentioned a building which overlooked the courtyard which had its blinds down. Unlike the other rooms which faced onto the play area, the children could not see in. He also described a piece of play equipment he didn't like: the bridge over the sand pit. John didn't like a particular part of the nursery because it reminded him of an incident that had disturbed him. He brought this incident into many of his answers to the child conferencing questions.

Activities

Children's response to questions about their best days in the nursery reflected different interests. A day out to the railway station had been popular. Children also mentioned games they had liked playing such as hide and seek, playing with construction toys and creative activities. In response to the question 'what do you find difficult?' Clare referred to writing. Written activities had not been mentioned by children in response to any other question. Gary mentioned the footpath on the way to nursery which had low-down branches.

Using child conferencing to listen to young children

Choose setting carefully We chose a familiar setting for the child conferencing. A table was set out in the corridor, a popular place in the nursery, with doors open into the courtyard. We set out paper and new felt-tip pens for children to draw a picture or map of the nursery. The children were at ease taking part in the child conferencing in this setting with the researcher. Practitioners may decide on different venues. The Head of TCECC had conducted child conferencing in her office. The children involved told her they felt important being asked what they thought, in her room.

Be flexible Child conferencing may need to be conducted on the move. Two boys began the interview session inside and then proceeded to show the researcher their favourite outdoor spaces. The interview then continued outside.

We were also flexible about how many children were involved at any one time. Some children asked to be interviewed with a friend. Others preferred to be interviewed individually. Child conferencing could be extended to form the basis of a group discussion or 'focus group'.

Be sensitive We wanted children to feel in control of the child conferencing and to be able to stop or not answer a question, at any time. We could have introduced a 'stop sign' or similar symbol for the children to indicate if they wanted to end or pause the conversation. We chose not to use this in this setting, but we made it very clear in our introduction to the conferencing that the children could stop answering at any time. We felt that the children were confident enough in their relationship with the researcher, built up over several months, to say if they didn't want to continue. Two of the seven children in the kindergarten group chose to end the interview before the last question: one boy said, 'I've had enough questions now'.

Take time The children who repeated the child conferencing after four months needed time to think about their previous responses. In this way child conferencing is a reflexive tool. Children needed to reconsider their previous answers, such as 'what do you find difficult?' and evaluate their present feelings. This can be a complex process but children who become used to being consulted will become more and more competent at using this skill. There is the likelihood that in every setting for young children, there will be some children who are confident at answering questions in this formal way and also others who will not be open to this method. One boy in the kindergarten group chose not to take part.

Cameras

Cameras are a medium which appeal to young children and provide a form of communication that is fun. We decided to introduce children's own photographs as one piece of the mosaic. There was the possibility of using photographs, taken by the researcher to form the basis of the interviews with children. However, we wished to develop work with pre-school children using the cameras themselves. This was one of the techniques used by the Daycare Trust (Daycare Trust, 1998) for children to photograph their 'favourite' things in nurseries. We have extended this approach to enable young children to provide a more in-depth view of life in their institution.

Cameras in action

Gary (three years) worked with a friend John (four years) on this activity. I gave the boys single use cameras and asked them to photograph important things in the kindergarten. The boys had seen several of the other children in the key group use cameras with me. They were both keen to have a try themselves. Gary's first photos were taken inside, of Gold room, Bronze room and the home corner in Silver room. There are several shots of the conservatory and the stacking tables and books.

The boys then wanted to go outside, so they put the cameras in the bags I had given them and they went outside to play. Here they took photos of the large trees by the fence, the 'cave', the hill and the space beside the sheds. Afterwards they had a turn on the bikes. Gary and John then joined Bob on a drawing table outside. Gary did a detailed Batman and Robin picture which he labelled. He was very pleased with himself for finding a way of attaching his picture to the wall outside. He took several photos of this and the other children working with Bob. His film ends with photos of John, the tunnel and the slide.

Researcher's field notes

The slide

The 'cave'

The shed

The big dark trees and a bike

Photographs taken of important things by Gary (age 3)

What did the use of cameras reveal about Children's perspectives of lives in the institution?

Children chose to photograph:

Friends	Keyworkers
Favourite play equipment	Hidden spaces
Display of days out	Own artwork
Trees	Furniture

We also investigated the possibility of older children (three and four years old) using cameras to record the lives of younger children in the nursery.

The value of using older children to teach younger children has been recognised in the child-to-child movement (Johnson and Ivan-Smith, 1995). Health has been the main emphasis of these programmes. Our study has more in common with the approach described by Langsted (1994: 31) in the Children as Citizens project where the expertise of older children was used to gather their perceptions of the lives of younger children. This could be described as a 'children about children' approach rather than child to child.

The advantage of this 'children about children' approach is that older children can call on their own experiences. These will not be the same as the very young children concerned but their perceptions maybe nearer than the best efforts of adults.

Clare and Meryl spent a morning in one of the nursery rooms where Meryl's sister, Toni (22 months) was based (see Case Study 1, page 38). The girls were asked to take photographs of important things in the 'baby room' to show what it was like for Diane (age 8 months) and Toni to come to the nursery.

These photographs served as a discussion point with the older children, the practitioners in that setting and the younger children's parents. It was the photographs which set the agenda for these conversations.

Toni washing with Cathy

The cots

Daisy playing with the water

The 'potties'

Photographs taken of the nursery by Clare (age 4) and Meryl (age 3)

What did the use of cameras reveal about older children's perspectives of younger children's lives in the institution?

Children chose to photograph:

Keyworkers with the children	Potties
Mattresses	Towels
Parents and visitors in the room	Play equipment
Changing area	Washing area
Cots	

Both Clare and Meryl concentrated on the personal items and routines in their photographs. Five of Clare's twelve photos featured the changing mat, the cot, the mattress and quilt, individually named towels and potties high up on a shelf. The keyworker was in three of the pictures and in one where she was involved in helping Toni wash her hands. An outside picture was the only one to concentrate on play equipment, even though the inside space also had many interesting looking play objects. Meryl also photographed other adults in the room; two parents and the Head of TCECC when she visited the room.

In this study, the older children did not talk directly about what they thought it was like for the younger children to be in the nursery but 'spoke' through their photographs. Washing, being changed and sleeping were all shown to be important. Practitioners were photographed with affection. The older children also managed to record a sequence of events in the nursery experienced by the younger children. In Diane's case this showed her looking full and sleepy after her last minute feed from her mother before she left in the morning, to printing with her keyworker and enjoying playing with the water. Toni was shown to be bouncing on the trampoline outside, playing on the mat, waiting at the table to paint and then painting and washing with her keyworker afterwards.

This exploratory use of older children to widen our understandings of the lives of younger children requires further study. There appears the possibility that taking photographs may be one way of enabling children, who are themselves still under five, tell adults more about the important things for the youngest children in an early childhood institution.

Using cameras to 'listen' to young children

Choosing cameras The use of digital cameras has huge potential in this field, but at present the cost of the technology will limit its use by young children.[3] Polaroid cameras have the advantage of producing instant results, but their size and the cost of the camera and film hinder their use by young children. Single use cameras are relatively straightforward to operate, even with the use of a flash. The quality of photographs produced is good, relative to cost. The disposable nature of the camera can enable adults to allow young

---

3   The reduction in the relative cost of digital cameras has led to their widespread use in schools and early childhood settings in the UK.

children to take control of the camera, without concerns about damage to expensive equipment. The size of a disposable camera also lends itself to use by young children. The cameras are small and light enough to be held easily or carried in a bag or pouch while children play. The images produced can be developed swiftly, using 'one hour' or overnight processing. This is important in order to maintain the interest of young children.

Sharing the photographs Cameras are fun to use with young children. Children can enjoy choosing what they want to photograph and seeing the results. This enjoyment can be shared with friends and siblings and also with adults.

Cameras offer young children the opportunity to produce a finished product in which they can take pride. Children who have seen members of their family take photographs, poured over family albums or looked at photographs in books and comics, know that photographs have a value in the 'adult world'. This is not always the case with children's own drawings and paintings. Photographs can offer a powerful new language for young children. It is a language that children can use to convey their feelings as well as information through 'the silent voice of the camera' (Walker, 1993).

We made an extra set of photographs for each child to take home. The second set was used to make an individual book about the nursery with each child.

Lengthy discussions took place with the children at this stage, to clarify what they had intended their photographs to be about and how they felt about the results. Listening was again important when children chose which photographs they wanted to be in their books.

Tours

Tours are one way to extend work with young children and cameras. Again, the idea has been to use participatory techniques to extend the ways adults listen to young children. Tours are led by the children. The tour or walk is an exploration of an early childhood institution guided by the children themselves. Children are not only in charge of the event but also of how it is recorded at the time and documented. This can be achieved by the children making an audiotape and deciding who has the clip mike, completing drawings and taking photographs. This information can then be used to make a map or model of the site, directed by the children's own photographs.

'Transect' walks (Hart, 1997), used in Participatory Rural Appraisal is a method of gathering detailed information about an environment from the people who live there: 'systematically walking with local guides and analysts through an area, observing, asking, listening, discussing, learning'. The physical nature of this process offers possibilities for exploring children's 'local knowledge' of their own environment. Langsted (1994: 35) adopted a similar approach in a Scandinavian study of children's lives. He describes what can be seen as a 'walking interview' with five year olds in the BASUN project. Children walked the interviewer through their day, explaining what happens where.

Tours in action

In order to gain Gary's perspective of the site I asked him to take me on a tour of the whole building. I explained to him I wanted to know more about which rooms he uses through the day. We took a mini tape recorder with us and Gary had a single use camera.

He started by the water tray in Gold room and then took me to the front door. He showed me the toys in the entrance hall he likes to play with. Gary then took me down to Purple room where his brother is. Gary took a photo of Robin and of his mattress. I asked Gary about Orange room. He told me about teatime and his favourite toy there. In each room we visited Gary was keen to get involved in an activity. We passed the playing room ('dancing room') and back to the kindergarten. Gary showed me the craft area in Silver room, took a photo and stopped to make a model. He ended the session joining in a book making activity with Bob.

Researcher's field notes

What did the tours reveal about children's perspectives?

Children visited and talked about:

Rooms they were allowed in

Rooms they weren't allowed in

Rooms where favourite activities happened

Rooms where 'favourite' people worked

Displays of their own work

Outside space

In-between spaces, e.g. corridors

Rooms where siblings 'lived'

Friends and practitioners

The act of walking and directing allowed the children to talk freely about their experiences of the Campus. This is a child-led way of talking which is far more alive than the sterile environment of a traditional interview room. The physicality and mobility of this technique can demonstrate children's priorities which might otherwise become lost. It can present a way of moving towards a child agenda for change.

Mapping

Mapping is one way of recording the information provided by children during tours of their institutions. Making a two-dimensional representation of a place is a difficult conceptual task for young children. We wanted to connect the children's physical experiences of their environment with map-making by using children's own photographs.

In the study children met with the researcher within a week of taking photographs on a tour, to review them and to make maps. (Making treasure maps was also a current feature of some of the children's imaginative play.) The children were excited to see their photographs for the first time. At this stage we also made clear to the children they would be given a full set of the photos to take home at the end of the session. The children then selected which places they wanted to show on their maps. The children also added drawings made during the tours together with new drawings and writing on the maps.

Maps in action

Map 1

Gaby, Meryl and Cathy chose seven of their photos and four drawings which they had made, during a tour of TCECC. The spaces they chose to illustrate were: the office, the front door, 'the dancing room' where music and movement took place, Orange room where children over four had lunch and Purple and Yellow room for children under two. They also chose photos of themselves.

Map 2

Cathy and Clare worked together on a map following their tour together. The spaces they chose to represent their institution were: the cook and the kitchen, the receptionist and the office, the staffroom, Cathy's key room where her key group meets and the view out of the back window, the 'fruit table' in the conservatory and a table in another key group room. Clare also chose a photo of her 'glitter picture' from her portfolio of work which she included in her tour.

What did the maps reveal about children's perspectives?

The children chose a range of important spaces in keeping with those revealed on the tours:

Rooms they were allowed in

Rooms they weren't allowed in

Rooms where favourite activities happened

Rooms where 'favourite' people worked

Displays of their own work

Outside space

In-between spaces, e.g. corridors

Rooms where siblings 'lived'

Friends and practitioners

Children also included objects on their maps, such as examples of their own work and photographs of their friends. The close correlation between the information gathered on the tours and the making of the maps supports the importance of these places to the children. The maps also helped to clarify individual children's priorities, by making visible the information gathered on the tours. The only map not to include the garden was made following a tour conducted by the children on a wet day. Spaces for particular activities were selected, such as the home corner and the water tray but 'inbetween' spaces such as the entrance hall and corridors were also selected. The children showed a fascination with rooms they were not allowed access to such as the staffroom and kitchen.

The maps also revealed the importance of people as well as spaces, for example Gary's map showing his brother and his key room. These maps seemed to support the impression that the children's understanding of their institution was based on who was there as much as on what happened where. This appeared to be the case for Cathy, whose keyworker was in almost all of the photographs on her map.

Using maps to 'listen' to young children

Talk and listen together We made audiotapes of the map making sessions. Listening to children describe or 'interpret' their photographs is an important stage in building up a map together. Listening to children as they chose which photographs to use also conveyed insights into their perspectives.

Gather other children's views Other children in the nursery were interested in the maps. The visual nature and scale of the maps on large sheets of card meant that they could easily be seen and discussed. The mapmakers were also keen to tell others about their work.

Role play

Role play is another tool to use in the Mosaic approach. In this study we began to explore its potential, using play figures. We introduced a set of small play figures and play equipment, similar to those found in the nursery, to children in one of the key groups for children under two. Toni (age 22 months) was a member of this group.

Role play in action

I brought in a collection of play people, with a cot, toilet, slide, buggies and a rocker, together with figures of different sizes, skin colours and gender.

Toni was playing in the sand tray. I went and joined her and introduced the slide. She was very interested in the slide and then she put the figures in the sand. We gave the figures names. Toni chose which one was going to be her. She played with the figures on the slide.

I talked to Toni about the nursery … 'shall we make this bit the playground', and then we looked at the photographs of Toni playing outside taken by her sister. Toni placed the adult and child figures in the buggies and put them all down the slide.

Researcher's field notes

Toni's interest in the pram and in the slide were echoed in other pieces of the mosaic (see Case Study 1).

There is the possibility that role play using figures could be could be extended with older children to tell their own narratives about life in the nursery. This could build on the work by Hodges and Steele (Steele and others, 1999), who have used a 'story stem' approach with adopted children, where children are given a scenario enacted with play figures and asked to complete the narrative.

Each tool described above provides a piece of the mosaic. We have demonstrated how this multi-method approach can lead to a variety of ways of listening to young children. We have shown how the 'voice' of the child here can mean one of a number of languages or methods of expression. Some of the material gathered may have an evaluative element, in the sense that children attach different values and effects to their experiences; other parts will not, but will say more, for example, about how children understand their early childhood institution and their experience there. Both elements have been important in this study.

Parents' perspectives

Stage 1 of the Mosaic approach involves both adults and children gathering information. This is not intended to replace or undervalue the children's own responses but to become part of the dialogue about children's lives.

The particular emphasis in this project on developing new methodologies for listening to young children has resulted in the majority of the limited time available being apportioned to documenting children's perspectives. However, interviews were conducted with the parents of five of the twenty children involved in the study. One method used for documenting parents' perspectives of children's lives was an interview schedule, similar to the child conferencing.

Two of the parents interviewed were parents of children under two who had been the focus of all-day observations. This provided an opportunity for parents to stop and review what they thought would signify a good or bad day for their children. This allowed parents to share their unique perspective about their children and to think about what they had gleaned about their children's day to day experiences of being in the nursery. The questions sound deceptively simple, but they are in fact hard to answer. There are few opportunities in our busy lives to pause, step back and consider what life is like for the young children in our care.

Mother of Diane aged 8 months

What do you think Diane feels about being at the nursery?
I think she's happy. She was hard to settle at seven months. It took her a month to settle. She is playing more now. Before I used to stay on. Ginny and Cathy (practitioners) are great.

What would be a good day for Diane at home?
To be able to play with toys by herself. She has breast milk at home.

What do you think would be a good day for Diane at nursery?
To see different toys, playing with different shapes and colours. She likes playing with the lentils. She hasn't painted before. There is lots she hasn't got at home.

What do you think would be a bad day?
If she was crying too much. If she was sick or not feeling too well and I would have to come. Otherwise she'd be OK.

Excerpt from Parent interview

The emphasis in this exchange is on the perceptions of everyday experience of being in the nursery. It also allows parents to step back and think about the different sections to their children's lives: at home and as part of an early years institution. There is room also to convey some of their interpretations of their children's feelings and needs, skills which can make the difference between a miserable or contented child.

Parent's perceptions become another piece of the mosaic, and as such are important in building up a picture of children's lives. This is particularly the case for pre-verbal children.

Practitioners' perspectives

We were concerned not to introduce a way of listening to young children which in turn disempowers and devalues the adults who are responsible for their ongoing care. Involvement of practitioners in the listening process is essential if this is to be more than an auditing exercise and to become instead one way of promoting the ongoing process of listening to children day by day.

Throughout the process we talked to practitioners about the children in their group. We discussed 'thumbnail' sketches of the children before beginning our observation. This information included factual details about age, gender and siblings and also the practitioner's impressions of activities the children enjoyed and their friends. As children began to take part in the different mosaic activities time was built in to discuss with practitioners the children's perceptions which are discussed in Stage 2.

Interview schedules were used with two of the practitioners responsible for babies and toddlers involved in the study. The examples below and on page 39 show an interesting parallel with the mothers' comments about their children.

Diane's keyworker

What do you think Diane feels about being at nursery?
She likes it now. She is more settled. She likes banging toys together. It's unusual for her to cry when her mother leaves. She started crawling between her (preliminary) visits to the nursery and starting. She likes being put down and gets animated with playing with things.

What would be a good day for Diane in the nursery?
Something sensory to put her hands in. Lentils ... she likes those. Musical things that she can shake. A trip to the garden. Lots of cuddles.

What do you think would be a bad day?
If she has not had enough sleep at home or nursery. If got a cold, so we're blowing her nose all the time ... she cries.

What sort of day do you think Diane had today?
Pretty good. Better afternoon than morning. She was tired when she came in this morning and ready for a sleep. She cried when I changed her this morning and giggled with the horse (plastic figure) this afternoon.

Excerpt from Keyworker interview

Both Diane's mother and keyworker mention a good day for her would involve something tactile, like playing with the lentils. Both also associate a bad day for Diane if she is feeling unwell, although the keyworker also mentions tiredness. This was also the case in the interview with the two practitioners working with Toni (see Case Study 1, page 38).

There is the possibility of exploring the use of different methods for practitioners and parents to form their views about young children's lives. The use of cameras, video recorders, tape recorders, diaries and drawing could be incorporated into the Mosaic approach for adults to use as visual and verbal tools to focus on the lives of young children.

Researcher's perspectives

We were keen throughout to acknowledge the role of the researcher as a 'visible' part of the process. The researcher discussed with parents, practitioners and children her perceptions of the children's lives in the nursery as the study progressed. Observation notes, field notes and photographs formed the basis of this reflection. Again images were an important tool in developing the researcher's perspective as well as the children's perspectives. The researcher's viewpoint becomes a further piece in the Mosaic approach, for discussion and interpretation.

Stage 1 of the Mosaic approach has been concerned with children and adults gathering documentation. In Stage 2 we describe how the pieces of the mosaic can be drawn together.

Stage 2
Piecing together information for dialogue, reflection and interpretation
Bringing the mosaic together

Pieces of the mosaic, gathered by adults and children, form the basis for Stage 2. Combining the narratives and images of these individual pieces brings a greater level of understanding about young children's priorities. For example, a child may tell us about an important place in the nursery, during child conferencing. His photographs may add weight to this statement. Discussion with parents and practitioners may add further insight or reveal misunderstandings which can be discussed together.

In this study dialogue about the documentation was shared in the following ways:

- between children
- between practitioners and researcher
- between older children and researcher
- between parents or parents and children and researcher
- between practitioner groups and researcher.

It is difficult to bring such a visual process alive on paper. We will attempt to do this by using material gathered about the lives of three of the children in the study: Toni, age 22 months and Gary and Gaby age three years. We have described some of the individual pieces of the documentation for each child earlier in Part 2. Now the separate pieces are brought together.

Pre-verbal children
Case Study 1: Toni (age 22 months)

Researcher's observation	Keyworker's interview	Parent's interview
Photographs by older child (sibling)	**Toni (22 months)**	Role play

We have drawn together the different pieces in the Mosaic approach to build up a picture of what appears to be important parts of Toni's life in the nursery.

Mother of Toni

What do you think Toni thinks about being in the nursery?
I think she really likes it.
She doesn't seem anxious when I come to pick her up.

What would be a good day for Toni at home?
She always plays with her sister.
She plays doll's houses.
She likes physical activity in the garden, with the trampoline, and books before bedtime.

What do you think would be a good day for Toni at nursery?
To have been in the garden.
She loves the water play … and painting. She doesn't do that often at home.
Being able to play with the same group, and the same person, Andrew.

How do you know what sort of day she has had?
She is sometimes tired, usually not.
I notice when she is hungry.

What do you think would be a bad day?
If the weather is wet, she gets fed up.

Excerpt from Parent interview

Practitioner's perspectives: Toni

What do you think Toni feels about being at nursery?
She didn't want anyone near her. She now listens a lot more. She really enjoys water and dolls. She is very aware of routine – like giving out clothes (before going outside) and mealtimes …

What would be a good day for Toni in the nursery?
She comes in happily. She isn't upset for too long. She is keen to be involved in all aspects of the day. Andrew and Toni have built up a good friendship.

Excerpt from Keyworker interview

During the all-day observation of Toni, she spent a high proportion of her time organising her own games with her dolls. At times these games involved the home corner and lentils which were laid out on a nearby table. She was upset when she discovered it was too wet to play outside. When the rain stopped, she enjoyed being pushed in the pushchair by Andrew.

Observation in action

At 10.15am Toni comes and gets her doll and takes her to the table. She 'feeds' her lentils from a spoon. Ginny–Toni: 'Are you feeding your baby, Toni?' Toni holds her baby to feed her and then lays her down on the table and carries on feeding her ... Cathy–Toni: 'Are you feeding your baby, Toni? She has eaten a lot. Look, Andrew, Toni is feeding her baby ... is she full up?' Toni goes and gets a large toy for her doll to sit on. Cathy: 'Do you want to use one of these chairs?' Toni looks delighted. She pulls the chair out and puts her doll in the chair and tries to do up the strap. Cathy watches and waits. Then Toni manages it.

Excerpt from researcher's field notes. Cathy and Ginny are keyworkers

Drawing together these comments from the parent's and keyworkers' interviews and from the all-day observation, the photographs taken by Toni's sister and Clare and from Toni's role play with the play figures, key themes emerged.

What appear to be important parts of Toni's life in the nursery?

Outside play in the garden, including the slide

Water play

Painting

Activities with keyworker

Playing with Andrew

Dolls

Familiar routines

The following table shows which pieces of the Mosaic approach revealed which information and which themes appeared most frequently (Key: ◆ material gathered using individual pieces of the Mosaic approach).

Toni	Observation	Role play	Photographs by sibling	Parent interview	Keyworker interview
Outside play	◆	◆	◆	◆	
Water play			◆	◆	◆
Painting	◆		◆	◆	
Activities with keyworker	◆		◆		◆ keen to be involved in all aspects of the day
Special friend	◆		◆	◆	◆
Dolls and prams	◆	◆		◆	
Routines	◆		◆ own mattress, quilt	◆	◆

In this case study, the Mosaic approach has helped to create a 'living picture' of life in the nursery for Toni. As Toni becomes more able to communicate her own views this picture can be expanded and changed. However, as this case study illustrates we do not need to wait until children can talk:

> Listening must not wait until children are able to join in adult conversations. It should begin at birth, and be adapted to their developing capacities for communication and participation in their social world.

> (Tolfree and Woodhead, 1999)

Children with speech

Case Study 2: Gary (age 3)

These different pieces of the mosaic, which Gary had been instrumental in gathering, were brought together to form a detailed picture of the important parts of his life in the kindergarten. The researcher first worked with Gary when he was three and a half years old and again five months later.

Gary conveyed the following priorities for his life in the nursery

Places to hide

Outside space for imaginative games

Time to play with his friend

The bikes

Grown-ups to keep order

Time for other places, family and friends

The following table shows which pieces of the mosaic revealed which information and which themes appeared most frequently (Key: ◆ material gathered using individual pieces of the mosaic).

Gary	Observation	Conferencing	Cameras	Tours	Maps	Parent	Practitioner
Places to hide	◆	◆	◆	◆	◆		
Imaginative games	◆	◆	◆	◆	◆	◆	◆
Playing with friends	◆	◆	◆	◆		◆	◆
Not playing with x		◆		◆			
Bikes	◆	◆	◆	◆	◆	◆	◆
Grown-ups keeping order		◆				◆	
Playing with his brother	◆			◆	◆		
Time outside the nursery				◆		◆	

These themes became the focus for dialogue, reflection and interpretation with Gary, his friends, his mother and his keyworker.

Imaginative play The child conferencing provided an interesting starting point for discussion. In July, Gary had named the slide as 'what he liked best' about the kindergarten. In November this had changed to: 'Going in my cave and working in the desert and listening to my music in my cave. It's very dark so I need my torch. It's a magic torch.'

This response was echoed in Gary's answer to where was his favourite place in the kindergarten: 'In my cave listening to music. It's magic music from my magic radio.'

Gary had then showed the researcher where the cave was during the tour he gave her of the site. It was a circular bench on a small piece of grass in the outside play area. He took a photograph of the cave and included it on his map.

Outside play The shed and the piece of 'forgotten' ground by the fence, round the back of the large trees, were featured in many of Gary's photographs.

Playing with friends John featured in many of Gary's photographs and in the corresponding questions in the child conferencing about people he liked.

Not playing with x Gary made it clear in the child conferencing that he didn't like a particular child. He also asked not to go on a tour with this child.

Bikes were another major feature of Gary's life When asked why he came to the kindergarten he answered: 'I come by bike.' He also drew a picture of a bike when invited to draw a picture about his kindergarten.

Order seemed to be very important to Gary He saw one job of grown-ups as to 'tell people off'. This linked to what he didn't like, being punched and hit by other children.

Playing with his brother Gary took the researcher on the tour to see his brother who was in the nursery wing of TCECC. The affectionate rapport they shared was apparent from their greeting.

Time outside of nursery While taking the researcher on the tour, Gary spoke of friends outside of the kindergarten and described the places he liked to visit (see tours section).

Dialogue with Gary's mother and keyworker made some of these impressions clearer, while in other instances revealed differences of perspective. Gary's mother confirmed the importance to Gary of his imaginative games, his best friend and his bike. These priorities did not appear to have changed significantly between July to November. Gary had a part-time place at nursery and she echoed the importance to the whole family of pursuing other interests, exploring other places together. Gary's keyworker commented on the importance of the outside space to Gary and his friends. His keyworker was surprised however at which child Gary was adamant he did not like.

Case Study 3: Gaby (age 3)

Gaby was one of the younger children in the kindergarten group. She showed great interest in using the camera and was involved in leading a tour, map-making and child conferencing. The researcher also interviewed Gaby's mother and her keyworker who were both involved in giving their own insights and in reflecting on Gaby's perspectives.

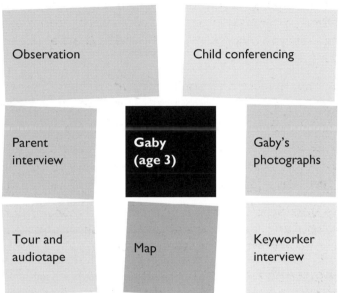

Gaby conveyed the following priorities for her life in the nursery:

Space to play with her friends, especially role play

Knowing which adults were there

Making things

Singing

Tasty food

The following table shows which pieces of the mosaic revealed which information and which themes appeared most frequently.

Gaby	Observation	Conferncing	Cameras	Tours	Maps	Parents	Practitioner
Friends and role play with friends	◆	◆	◆	◆	◆	◆	◆
Adults being there						◆	
Making things		◆	◆	◆			
Singing		◆	◆	◆	◆	◆	
Tasty food		◆				◆	
Wish to join in with four year olds				◆	◆	◆	

Playing with friends was a vital part of Gaby's day in the kindergarten This was apparent from the first observations the researcher made of her (see 'Observation', pages 15–18). The significance of being able to play together, especially in elaborate role play, was reinforced by Gaby through her responses to the child conferencing in both sessions five months apart, and also in her photographs. Almost every photo showed a child or children, but no grown ups. In the photographs Gaby selected for her book about the kindergarten she chose friends standing by the slide, the sand pit, the cooker, outside in the garden by the climbing frame. Unlike Gary, she didn't appear interested in the shed or the fence at the back of the garden.

Her friends had changed in between the times the researcher carried out the child conferencing with Gaby. Her best friend was still the same girl but another girl was no longer there: 'She's not my friend now because she is at big school.'

Adults being there It was difficult to tell from Gaby's responses to child conferencing and from her photographs and observation what importance she attached to the adults in the nursery. They didn't feature in many of her photographs and she appeared to spend as much time as possible with her friends. When asked 'what should grown-ups do at the kindergarten?' Gaby replied: 'play with people'. Discussion with Gaby's mother made clearer Gaby's feelings about the practitioners. Her mother had asked Gaby: 'If you feel down or sad who would you like to go to?' Gaby said 'Nina or Bob' (her keyworker). Gaby's mother explained that Gaby is very fond of Bob: 'In the first six months he was her security'. This made it difficult for Gaby when she found out that Bob is on a term time contract whereas Gaby comes all year: 'That was a big issue for her'.

Making things Gaby chose a photograph of herself and a friend playing with the play dough for her book about the kindergarten. Gaby described her best day in Bob's group, during the child conferencing as: 'Sticking paper on balloons and you rip it and stick it on balloons.' Bob was surprised that Gaby and Clare had both described mask making with the papier mache as their favourite day in his group – he thought they had found it arduous! This reinforced for Bob *the need to ask children rather than assume what they think.*

Singing Gaby loved to sing. Her favourite spot in the kindergarten was the 'fruit place' in the conservatory, 'we always do singing here'. Another place for music was the 'dancing room' which Gaby and her friends took the researcher into on their tour of the kindergarten and also chose to illustrate on their map. Gaby's mother confirmed that Gaby enjoyed singing: 'she sings at home a lot. She wants to be a singer.'

Tasty food Gaby thought the food in the kindergarten was 'yummy, yummy, yummy'. She took a photograph of the kitchen on the tour. Food was also an important social event at home as well. Gaby's mother valued the variety of food on offer. She described Gaby as part of a multicultural family where the diversity of food reflected her rich cultural background. Gaby's mother saw the kindergarten as also reflecting this diversity.

The wish to join in with the four year olds This information had not become obvious from the child conferencing, observations or the photographs Gaby initially took. However, on the tour Gaby took the researcher into Orange room where the four year olds have their lunch. Meryl, her four-year-old friend, told the researcher in great detail what happens at lunchtime in this room. Gaby sat there quietly and listened and then talked to the researcher about how much she was looking forward to being able to have lunch in here: 'I can't wait to get big'. Gaby later chose a photograph of Orange room for the map she made with her friends. Her mother also confirmed Gaby's desire to be older, including daily conversations about going to school.

These case studies illustrate the value of young children using more than one tool to communicate their ideas. Some views and desires are harder for young children to express than others. Friends for example can be captured on camera but liking role play is harder to convey. Adult observations and discussions with practitioners and parents can add further details which can clarify our understandings of children's priorities.

This approach also allows for differences of perception to be made visible. Different perspectives documented by parents, practitioners and children can provide the basis for useful discussions and 'meaning making'. For example, in Case Study 3 above, the importance of adults to Gaby's life in the nursery was emphasised much more strongly by Gaby's mother than by Gaby herself through the other tools used. This may indicate that Gaby's priorities have moved on. Discussing such apparent contradictions are central to deepening our understanding of children's views and experiences of their early childhood institutions.

Reflection into practice

The material gathered in this study was used as part of an evaluative dialogue with practitioners of TCECC, looking at what it is like for children to be in this place. Firstly, the researcher discussed with practitioners the materials gathered by the children, including documentation about the babies. These in turn formed questions for further reflection and action.

We began by discussing the questions the researcher had formed from working with Gary and reflecting on the documentation.

Reflective questions based on documentation

Do you give me space to hide?

Do you let me play on the grass?

Do you give me time to make up my own games?

Do you let me play on the bikes?

Do you allow me to see my brother?

Do you ask me what I think before changing the garden?

Two particular issues were taken as points for future action:

- wider consultation with children about the use of outside spaces;
- structures within the centre for siblings to play together.

Discussions also considered the more fundamental question of how listening to young children can increase, among so many other agendas.

Recognising the unexpected

Using participatory techniques with young children enables their priorities and concerns to be the starting point for change. These may be different from those of adults.

We began our analysis with a list of possible themes chosen by the Daycare Trust (1998) in their recent study of listening to young children: friends, food, finding out, outside play and grown-ups. 'Conflict' was added to this list based on earlier observations carried out on the site. Did this initial list correspond with the details children chose to document?

- Friends and changing friendships were a repeated feature of the child conferencing and the photographs. This included details about friends' shoes and friends' hairstyles. 'Grown-ups' featured in children's lists of people they liked. Ideas were expressed about adults' roles keeping order and playing with the children.

- Food did not feature as a major concern; however, the kitchen, as well as the cook, was recorded by the children as an important place in the kindergarten during one of the tours. The conservatory where fruit and milk were shared was also mentioned as a favourite place.
- 'Finding out' is a theme used by the Daycare Trust to describe the activities children can take part in. These were not a major feature of the children's documentation. Some children mentioned and photographed books. Others described creative activities as their favourite part of being in the kindergarten. This was mentioned more by girls than boys.
- Outside play and the environment in general, including the large trees that overlooked the play area, were described by the majority of the children. The maps made emphasised the outside play space (apart from when rain prevented photos being taken outside).
- Conflict and how it was dealt with by practitioners did prove to be a concern of the children. This was revealed through the child conferencing where children remarked on the importance of having adults around to 'tell people off'. Physical conflict was the main reason mentioned for not liking other children. Adults did not appear in the list of people children did not like.

Our study also revealed concerns and interests about:

- Feelings about the past and future. Some children displayed this by telling the researcher about friends who had left. This also extended to memories about adults who were no longer working in the kindergarten. One very shy child, while taking the researcher on a tour asked to have her photograph taken by a photograph of her keyworker who had recently left to have a baby. It was apparent that she still felt a great deal of affection for her keyworker, who remained an important part of the kindergarten for this child.

The children also raised discussions about the future. Orange room in particular prompted such conversations, as we have seen from Gaby (see Case Study 3, page 45). This room had acquired a status that the researcher was unaware of as a visiting adult, as only four year olds had their lunch in this room.

We have concentrated in this account on the young children in the kindergarten and nursery of TCECC. At the same time as conducting this fieldwork the researcher was involved in a pilot study of the

Mosaic approach with refugee children in Field Lane Homeless Families Centre. The short time span of this project has resulted in this part of the study being more exploratory, raising questions about the possibilities of using the Mosaic approach in such a setting.

Mosaic approach with refugee children

There are particular groups of young children whose circumstances may render them more invisible and powerless than others of their age group. In referring to children in this way we do not want this to be a denial of difference and individuality. However, there are external factors which make the particular issues around listening to children in their circumstances worthy of additional consideration. Refugee children are one such group whose past experiences of forced migration and current circumstances mean it is more imperative for adults to listen and harder to accomplish.

The range of languages spoken other than English is the most obvious 'barrier' to listening. Interpreter support in a number of different languages is essential if practitioners are going to be able to listen to young refugee children. Working closely with parents is another important link not only in the mechanical process of communicating but also in gaining an understanding of the children's past experiences and of what is important to them. Last but not least, some refugee children may be suffering the effects of trauma, having experienced loss in many forms whether of family, friends, familiar places, objects or routines.

Communication under these circumstances can benefit from specialist techniques such as play therapy (Cattanach, 1997). There is not necessarily the expertise or resources for those working with refugee children to use such an approach.

Gathering documentation in action

I explained to Sasha I was making a book about the Campus and wondered if she could help me. I started off with a few questions about what she liked doing when she came to Field Lane.

I like drawing houses. I like playing with the jigsaws. I like jumping on the bouncer. I like playing in the house because it has got lots of things.

Then I explained about taking photographs of things she liked at the centre.

Sasha approached the task very carefully. She appeared quite nervous at first about taking a photo. She took one first of all of the playhouse … and was obviously relieved when the flash went off and she had taken her first photo.

She wanted to take photos inside first … she was very aware of the displays. She took one of the Halloween display. She photographed the alphabet poster which was very high up and stretched around the room. She took the poster in careful stages, starting with wxyz.

Sasha asked to go outside although the door was locked at the time and took photos of the yard and of the garden.

Inside she asked to take a photo of her mother and then a family friend asked that she take a photo of her son. She didn't want me to take a photo of herself.

The centre was celebrating a birthday with a cake and sandwiches so Sasha took a few photos of the food.

Sasha was interested in how many photos she had left to take and decided to take the last photos of the grown-ups chatting in the main room and the last photo of a younger girl.

Researcher's field notes

What did the use of cameras reveal about these refugee children's perspectives?

The children chose to photograph:

Friends

Family members

Shared meals

Playspace

Outside space

Practitioners and researcher

Wall displays

There were certain parallels between the material gathered by children in Field Lane and the responses of children in the kindergarten. Friends, and particularly those of the same nationality were important. The outside space was precious, despite being very small. Practitioners photographed and talked about were not limited to the 'crèche' where children spent some of their time, but to adults throughout the centre. One of the children also photographed members of her family who were also at the centre.

Developing the Mosaic approach to work with refugee children

Our limited use of the Mosaic approach with refugee children suggests that this may be an area for future development for the following reasons:[4]

View of the child: children as experts in their own lives This competent model of the child may have particular relevance where children are seen as being the victim of difficult circumstances. While not seeking to deny the trauma these children may have experienced, this approach starts from a position of recognising their skills in being themselves.

---

4   See the work of Tony Bertram and Chris Pascal in this area (for example Bertram and Pascal, 2009).

Concrete and visible The Mosaic approach emphasis on the here and now may help to draw attention to children's current experiences. This may be important in circumstances where these may become lost among the pressing needs of adults.

'Hundred languages' The ability to use visual and other methods which do not rely on the written word may be a particular strength when working with children for whom English is an additional language. There is also the possibility that children could work in their preferred language, so the Mosaic approach could be built up in more than one language. This demonstrates its flexibility.

Participatory Children have the opportunity to take control and record reality as they see it at a time when they and their relatives are seen as powerless.

Fun The use of imaginative tools may provide a release from stressful circumstances. The use of cameras for example can be great fun and satisfying to use. This may also provide new ways for children to communicate how they feel. Tolfree describes the benefit of 'playful techniques' with children facing trauma (Tolfree, 1996).

One of the disadvantages of using this approach with refugee children is that building up a mosaic takes time. There is the possibility that children who are in temporary housing may move on at little or no notice. This does not render the approach unworkable but places the emphasis on each piece of the mosaic such as child conferencing or use of a camera having value for the child in itself. A platform for listening can be provided but this may be less complete than might be the case if children were in a less mobile environment. There is also the important issue of privacy which applies not only to refugee children but may be of particular relevance here. Children may disclose information about their past or current circumstances that it would be inappropriate or insensitive to display in a public way. This may mean that the Mosaic approach becomes more of an individual tool in this situation.

Summary

We have described a portfolio of tools that can be used and adapted for working in particular settings. However, the portfolio is an open one. New tools can be added according to adults' and children's skills and interests. The important ingredients are, first the methods: the combined use of tools which enable young children to express their ideas and feelings with confidence. Second, it is the attitude towards children which this approach represents: children as experts in their own lives. Third, there is a value in each piece of the mosaic. However, the value is increased by combining with other pieces or perspectives, including those of parents and practitioners.

The assembling of data is not the end of the process but forms the beginning of reflexive interaction in which children, practitioners, parents and researchers can engage to interpret and negotiate meanings. Apparent contradictions, changes in perspective and incomprehension can be discussed together. This can lead to a reassessment of what life is like in a particular early childhood institution for young children and form the basis for ongoing conversations.

We have described the Mosaic approach as a way of gaining young children's perspectives of their daily lives. The Mosaic approach in use in an educational setting also extends consultation beyond a learning agenda. Exchanges between practitioners and parents can have a focus which is not necessarily dominated by educational progress and starts from the child's perspective. It is in the interpretation of the material gathered that the possibility for greater understanding of young children's lives will emerge.

Part 3
Possibilities and
challenges of listening

Part 3 raises some of the possibilities and challenges of listening through research using the Mosaic approach in early childhood institutions.

First, in what ways can this approach to listening to young children be taken up in an early childhood institution? Will this reflexive model enable practitioners to gain new understandings about the priorities of children's lives? How will these insights be used? Can this approach benefit the children who are consulted in this way? Could this approach lead to young children's competencies being employed to better effect in day to day decision making?

Second, what are the potential challenges of listening? At the time of writing the first edition this was a reminder of the need to adopt a critical approach. This has become increasingly important among the changing shifts of political favour. Our intention is not to dissuade practitioners from seeking new approaches to listening, but to remain alert to possible difficulties and unintended consequences. The complexities of listening to young children are ongoing, questions of interpretation and power continue. What may change is the political context in which this level of in-depth communication between young children and adults is taking place.

Third, what conditions are necessary for the Mosaic approach to be taken up? What prerequisites are there in terms of practitioners' attitudes and skills, timing and resources? What demands does such an approach place on the children who take part? How can this way of relating to young children support a culture of listening in which adults and children's views and experiences are valued?

Possibilities of listening

The following examples are possible ways of extending the use of the Mosaic approach with young children.

Individual reviews

Children could be asked about what is important to them about their early childhood institution. This visual and verbal material could be collected and displayed in order to form the focus of discussion between the child, the parents and practitioners. Photographs taken by the children could be included in individual records or portfolios, together with copies of the child conferencing.[1] The participatory methods would allow these exchanges to begin from the child's perspective. Priorities provided by the child could be discussed alongside a more learning-orientated agenda. This material frequently could be returned to with the children to aid their own reflection and reassessment of life in the early childhood institution.

Internal audits

Practitioners could use the Mosaic approach with a sample of children from each key group to review what are children's priorities in the early childhood institution and how has this changed over time. This material could be discussed collectively to reflect together on what children are saying. This could be compared with practitioners' own experience of the same environment. In displaying their priorities children may also reveal what parts of daily life are not seen as important. Children in this study, for example, did not talk about the computer or language groups. An exploration of such issues may lead to further discussion with children to see if these activities are just taken for granted or need to change to increase children's interest.

---

1   Driscoll and Rudge (2005) explain how profile books, ongoing 'living' records of individual children became central to the listening culture at their children's centre.

Changes to the environment

The Mosaic approach has been used in this study to explore children's use of the space in early childhood institutions. There is the possibility that this way of listening to young children could be used before outside or inside space is reordered.[2] In the study a clear picture was built up about the importance of unstructured spaces for children. Plans to change an outside play area could incorporate using the Mosaic approach with one key group to see what they enjoyed about the space or would like to change. The oldest children in an institution could in turn be involved in recording younger children's use of the space by taking photographs, or by interviewing other children. The material gathered in such an exercise could be displayed in a public space such as an entrance hall so parents and other practitioners could share their interpretations.

A similar process could be used to gather children's perspectives about a particular room or inside space, for example a home corner. Children may reveal very different perspectives from adults about the uses or associations of a certain room.

Such insights could inform the decision-making process as to future changes for the space.

Ongoing dialogue

In addition to the specific possible uses for the Mosaic approach, this also represents another way of promoting the ongoing dialogue between children, practitioners and parents. Such a process would be in addition to existing opportunities, used in early childhood institutions to gain children's perspectives such as during Circle Time at the beginning and end of the day. The Mosaic approach could be developed as a framework for reinforcing the importance of listening to young children about the quality of their lives.

---

2   These ideas have been explored further in subsequent studies (see Appendix)

Listening using the Mosaic approach: day nursery example

Gathering perspectives

Practitioners at Patacake Day Nursery have worked with the Mosaic approach to review with young children what it is like to be a child in their settings. This has included a review carried out in the summer term with the oldest children in the nursery before the children start school. Firstly, children are introduced to taking their own photographs. This nursery has found it useful to work first with a small group of the more confident children who are happy to take photographs of their likes and dislikes within the nursery. These photographs become the catalyst for child conferencing with the children who took the photographs. These conversations are then opened out to include a wider group of children. The photographs are sometimes made into a collaborative map of, for example a classroom or the garden. Children's photographs, drawings and comments can then be added to this shared document.

Introducing the Mosaic approach to practitioners

The decision was taken by the Manager to introduce her colleagues to the Mosaic approach by holding a training evening in which she gave the practitioners experience of trying out an adaptation of some of the research activities or tools for themselves. Dividing into three groups, one group took digital photographs of the nursery, a second group filled out a short questionnaire and a third group constructed maps of the nursery. Each activity focused on the spaces practitioners enjoyed working in and those they felt less comfortable. An important part of the training session was allowing time for the groups to listen to each other's perspectives. This provided a helpful illustration of how to work with young children using the Mosaic approach.

Listening to babies

This nursery has explored different ways of building of a mosaic of perspectives about the youngest children. This has posed some of the greatest challenges as the younger the child the more assumptions might need to be made about their experiences. Practitioners adapted the idea of the tour. The practitioners used tracking observations to follow how babies reacted and interacted in different areas of the nursery, with different people and activities. The importance of listening to body language was emphasised. These detailed observations were added to discussions with parents and with key persons and other practitioners who added different perspectives on their impressions of what being in the nursery was like for these babies.

Listening to young children with additional needs

This nursery has drawn on the expertise of peers to help build up a mosaic about the experiences of young children with additional needs within the setting. This included a child who did not use verbal communication in the nursery. The manager drew on the observations of his peers about his play. The children took photographs of his play with the manager, who was also his key person. The photographs showed the activities he regularly selected and enjoyed. These photographs became the focus of discussions with his peers about where they felt were the positive and negative places in the nursery for their friend. These perspectives were added to those of the manager, to observations and to the comments of his parents.

Patacake Day Nursery, Cambridge. Further details are covered in the Open University Foundation Degree (Module: Extending Professional Practice in the Early Years (E210)).

Listening using the Mosaic approach: pre-school example

Research linked to training

Two members of Surrey County Council's Early Years and Childcare team carried out a research study at Worplesdon Pre-school as part of the development of training material for childcare providers on listening to young children. The project took place over a three-month period, focusing on 6 children, across the age range at the setting: 2 years 9 months to 5 years. Additional activities were added to enable all children to participate in thinking about what they enjoyed about being at pre-school. The following research tools were included in the study: observations, photo tours, child conferencing, mapmaking, interviews with parents and key persons and compiling a chart of favourite equipment and places in the setting.

What worked well?

Voice recordings were made while observing the children's use of the space. These were transcribed and written up as narrative observations. Children used child-friendly digital cameras, working in pairs, in groups or individually accompanied by an adult. The older children were able to take their own photographs after instruction and produced some meaningful images with clear explanations of their choices. Most of the children enjoyed reviewing the images they had taken, which had been organised into individual albums. These images were used as prompts for the discussion in the child conferencing. Children worked with their own photographs and craft material in the mapmaking session, dictating their comments to adults. Children added drawings to the map of important features not included on the photo tour. Interviews with parents added a different perspective on children's experience of the setting. Interviews with the children's key persons provided a balance to the material gathered in other sessions.

How the methods could be improved?

Reflections for improvement having worked with the individual research tools included: increasing the types of observation carried out to include tracking observations of different places in the setting as well as observations of individual children; building in time for children to familiarise themselves with cameras prior to starting the project; introducing video as well as still images; using a laptop or computer to review images and including a review of a child's learning journey in interviews with key persons.

Issues to consider

The time needed to listen, transcribe and analyse the material gathered was emphasised, for example in undertaking detailed observations. A template to record details of the tour was recommended (see Clark, 2010a: 55). Time and resources to print and collate images was raised, leading to suggestions to review some images on screen before children made choices as to which to print.

This case study is used in training on listening to young children to act as a catalyst for settings to think about their own assumptions about children's choices.

Listening using the Mosaic approach: children's centre example

Background

Treetops Children's Centre focused on listening to young children using the Mosaic approach to reflect on 'what it is like for a child in this setting?'. The centre chose the following research tools: practitioner observations and reflections, walking tours, mapmaking, drawing, craftmaking and photography, individual interviews with children and whole group discussions during Circle time.

This was part of a wider project in Gloucestershire on listening to young children supported by the Young Children's Voices Network.[3]

Outcomes

The participatory tools revealed children's knowledge about place use as well as place feelings (Clark, 2004). Children defined different spaces in the setting according to their association with activities, objects, resources and people. Children's drawings, photographs and comments emphasised the small world area, role play area, painting area and nursery garden. Children also drew attention to areas where their favourite activities took place or where their special toys could be found.

This group of pre-school children (the oldest children in the centre) showed particular interest on the tour when they went into the rooms of the younger children: the 'Rising 3s'. Some of the older children had only recently left these rooms and had strong attachments to the space as well as to the practitioners and children. Some of the children also had siblings in this room.

Favourite people featured frequently and their associations with particular places. All of the children were able to articulate clearly who were their favourite peer or adult. Children's representations, photographs and comments emphasised the importance of being at pre-school and having a friend to play with. Display boards were photographed and in particular one near the mark-making area which was one where the children could display their own work. A photograph was also taken of photographs on display of themselves in a nearby nature area.

Ways forward

Practitioners observed that children became more competent at expressing their views and preferences with each opportunity. This accumulative effect emphasised the need for time, space and patient adults in order for children's perspectives to be collected. This project underlined for the practitioners the importance of embedding listening to children as part of everyday practice and not just a way of working that is 'parachuted in'.

The children's centre commented that using the Mosaic approach whilst working together as a group enhanced the milieu for listening, sharing knowledge and preferences and constructing meanings.

---

3   Young Children's Voices Network (YCVN) promotes listening to and participation with children from birth to five at a local and national level in England and is based in the Early Childhood Unit of the National Children's Bureau: www.ncb.org.uk/ycvn

What are *the benefits for children* of using this approach? This small study suggests that there is the potential for the following wide ranging benefits for young children who are listened to in this way.

Increasing confidence

Primarily, the Mosaic approach regards children as experts in being children. Listening to children's views and experiences in this way conveys that adults believe they have something to learn from children, which may be a boost to the children's confidence. Children involved in this study appeared to display an increasing confidence in expressing their views as the study progressed. This was the case for reserved children as well as the more articulate ones. For example, one of the practitioners remarked on the increasing confidence of Cathy who was a very shy child. She had taken great pleasure in taking her own photographs and making her maps. Here the use of a variety of methods including the visual tools is an advantage.

Developing skills

Increasing confidence is linked to pleasure in developing new skills. This multi-method framework represents the opportunities for young children to try new ways of expressing their views and feelings. In this study this was repeatedly demonstrated by the children's developing confidence in using the camera. These new skills may also increase children's competencies at home and in other settings as well. For example, several children in the study had requested cameras to use at home. Gaby's mother described the pleasure Gaby's father felt in being able to share her new interest in photography. Opportunities to develop new technical skills are also matched by the chance to extend cognitive skills too. The Mosaic approach encourages children as well as adults to be reflexive and reflect on what is important to them. In discussing the importance of listening to children Tolfree and Woodhead (1999: 21) describe this developing skill:

> It's not so much a matter of eliciting children's preformed ideas and opinions, it's much more a question of enabling them to explore the ways in which they perceive the world and communicate their ideas in a way that is meaningful to them.

Becoming more active participants

The benefits of being engaged in this way may have longer-term effects on how children view themselves in their early years environment. Further research is necessary here but this study suggests that some of the children involved were more able to engage with the day to day life in the kindergarten following the study. Gaby's keyworker described the Mosaic approach as providing a means for Gaby to access the curriculum more widely. She had become 'more of an active participant'. This participation could be in terms of day to day choices and involvement in the life of the early childhood institution or decision-making about wider changes.

Challenges of listening

This study has explored different ways of listening to young children. We are advocating the use of creative methods to consult young children about their views and experiences. We have also become aware of certain potential pitfalls in listening, through the process of carrying out this work, talking to practitioners and reviewing the literature. We include these questions as points for discussion for those planning this type of work.

Do we respect young children's privacy?

Listening is not a right. There needs to be space to respect children's need for privacy, while opening channels for communication for all those who wish to do so. One three year old said during the study, as he drew the child conferencing session to an early close: 'I've done enough talking now.' We need to be aware that listening can be a liberating tool but also a way of 'listening in' on children's lives and an unwanted intrusion.

What are the consequences of listening for young children?

There is the risk that listening to young children about their lives becomes part of a regulatory agenda, used to control children. The 'visible child' may be more easily controlled. More knowledge about young children's use of 'free time' may open up these spaces for more prescribed curriculum input. However, if adults chose to use this information in a different way, the 'visible child' can be a more respected child. Greater insights into young children's priorities could lead to more freedom for children to explore these priorities.

What are the consequences of listening for adults?

Listening to young children may also lead to more regulatory control of those with responsibility for children. Material made public through the documentation process with young children could be taken and used in a management context to control how time with children is spent. It is vital that children's perceptions gathered in a participatory way are not used to disempower practitioners but as a way of discussing meanings and changing practice together. The purpose behind the Mosaic approach is not to make children's knowledge unquestionable but to raise it to such a level that children's knowledge about their own lives is central to adult discussions.

What are the policy and financial pressures on listening?

There have been a proliferation of government policy initiatives which set out to listen to or consult with children including Quality Protects and Childcare Audits. This policy 'popularity' has not been without difficulties. Often these consultations needed to be carried out within tight timeframes. This put restraints on the type of listening which could take place. Funding was sometimes linked to demonstratable levels of consultation. In this context listening can become a compulsory activity. This may be at odds with our first question: do we respect young children's privacy?

Periods of financial restraints may result in listening to the perspectives of users declining in policy interest. The impact may be that posts created to facilitate listening to children are withdrawn at the same time as services being reduced. This increases the challenge on individual settings to maintain a culture of listening rooted in ongoing everyday practice.

How do we measure the effectiveness of our listening?

In a desire to prove to funders or employers that we have listened to young children there is a pull towards easily quantifiable measures: 'we have interviewed x number of children or held x number of focus groups'. In this climate too, the interpretative nature of listening can be easily overlooked. It is far harder to show that the culture within which we are working and the practice of that work, have changed in a way which respects children's skills and views more readily. This does not convert conveniently to neat graphs and tables but new ways need to be found to record these qualitative differences.

Conditions for listening

What needs to be in place in order for young children's perspectives to be taken more into account? Many of the factors discussed below will already be central to early years practice.

Climate of listening

We referred in Part 1 to the importance of a cultural climate which values children's opinions. This fundamental desire to listen to and involve children is a necessary prerequisite if children's views and experiences are going to influence the everyday relationships between adults and children in early childhood institutions. Nutbrown (1996: 55) advocates such a climate in the phrase 'respectful educators—capable learners':

> Adults with expertise who respectfully watch children engaged in their process of living, learning, loving and being are in a better position to understand what it is these youngest citizens are trying to say and find ways of helping them to say it.

The use of the Mosaic approach may be one way in which to help adults and young children to reflect together on this process of 'living, learning, loving and being'.

This climate of listening does not exist in a vacuum. How children are viewed at home is of course pertinent to a debate about listening to young children. Understanding differences and similarities in approach between parents and an early childhood institution are part of the everyday exchanges between practitioners and parents, for example Pascal and Bertram (1997).[4] The Pen Green Centre in Corby is one early years setting where the need to openly discuss differences has promoted a climate of listening. Practitioners used group discussions with parents to explore differences between rules, boundaries and level of choice offered to children at home and in the nursery.

Such discussions would be a useful starting point for introducing the Mosaic approach, which in turn could foster this climate of listening, in which the views of parents, practitioners and young children are respected and differences can be debated.

Taking time to listen

Listening to young children cannot be a rushed activity. The younger the child the less able and desirable it is to rely on direct questions. A short questionnaire may be the quickest way of asking children what they think about a place, but more information will be gained about children's perspectives from spending time using a multi-method approach. The Mosaic approach involves a time commitment for early years practitioners in a number of ways:

- Gathering the material will take longer because we are not relying on a single method of communication. Individual children may take longer than others to use a particular tool. For example, in the study several children took a film of photographs in half an hour whereas other children took several hours to take fewer photos.
- Interpreting the material gathered is time-consuming. Negotiating meanings is a valuable part of the process which involves practitioners taking time out to reflect on their own perceptions. There are no shortcuts available. There is the additional complexity of comparing material which is text-based with visual sources. Keeping children's perspectives central in this process requires patience, constantly engaging the children at each stage to check that meanings have not

---

4   Chris Pascal and Tony Bertram continue to make significant contribution to debates around listening to young children and parents, particularly in working with migrant, travelling, asylum-seeking and refugee families. This contribution has been both methodological and epistemological (see Pascal and Bertram, 2009). Children Crossing Boundaries project (Bertram and Pascal, 2008a) and Opening Windows programme (Bertram and Pascal, 2008b) demonstrate how knowledge gained through research with young children can become embedded in early childhood practice.

been assumed. Working in a way which includes the voices of parents alongside children and practitioners also requires time. Displaying material in a way which makes listening to young children's views and experiences more open also takes longer than recording one written record.

There is a serious need for more non-contact time for practitioners in early years childhood institutions in the UK. Listening to young children using the Mosaic approach requires space for practitioners to think and reflect.

Training

Listening to young children's perspectives is a skilful task which requires awareness raising and training. As Curtis (1996) comments, there are many different agendas in the various types of training programmes for working with young children among which the rights of the child may become submerged.

Training in child development is obviously an important prerequisite for understanding how young children communicate. The value of this training is increased where adults are trained to have 'wide eyes and open minds' (Nutbrown, 1996: 45), starting from the viewpoint of children as competent learners with much to teach as well as to receive. This attitude is relevant to those engaged in training across the early years sector including teacher training, Early Years Professional Status and the National Vocational Qualifications in childcare and education.

The use of the Mosaic approach also raises questions about in-service training. Practitioners need to feel confident in offering a range of different 'languages' for children to choose to express themselves. Specific workshops may be needed to expand the range of tools on offer in a setting, for example to look at participatory methods such as mapping and walks, or to consider a tool for younger children such as the camera. Many of these ideas are familiar parts of everyday life in an early years setting. The added dimension here is how we can use these tools to further understand what sense children make of their lives.

The use of documentation as described in Stage 1 and Stage 2 of this report may also raise opportunities for training. This open way of recording and debating children's views and experiences may challenge more individual, outcome-orientated styles of record keeping.

Access by children

What conditions are needed for young children to be involved in the Mosaic approach? This study suggests that there is potential for children of different ages and abilities to participate in this way. We have included a case study in this report to describe how this framework could be used with babies. This beginning suggests that there are possibilities of developing this framework with parents, practitioners and older siblings of children under one year.

The flexibility of the approach also allows methods to be adapted by practitioners to suit the needs and interests of the young children in their care. In this study, this led to child conferencing being adapted to work 'on the move' with Gary and his friend while they played outside.

The multi-sensory nature of the methods make this approach of potential value in listening to the views and experiences of disabled children.[5] In this study, one of the original members of the key group, Charlie, had been identified as having possible autistic tendencies and had limited speech. Charlie featured in several of the photos taken by the other children and by the researcher. Charlie also in time signalled that he wanted to use the camera and he took a photograph of himself. These photographs were made into a book for Charlie about the kindergarten, and could provide the starting point for further conversation. Other tools could be added such as objects of importance from the institution to promote dialogue (Marchant, 1999). Tours could be led by a physically disabled child working independently or with an able-bodied peer.

The day nursery case study (see pages 59–60) indicates some imaginative ways of adapting the approach to include the experiences of babies and disabled children.

---

5   See Tangen (2008).

Adapting the Mosaic approach with young disabled children

Alice Paige-Smith and Jonathan Rix (2011) built on and adapted the Mosaic approach in a study of the perspectives and experiences of two families with a young child identified as having Down's Syndrome.

The aim of the study was to explore each family's perspectives on participating in an Early Intervention programme. The researchers began by carrying out detailed narrative observations supported by taking photographs of the children's favourite objects and activities during play. These photographs and accounts of the observations became the catalyst for discussions with the parents. These images were also shared with the children, whose verbal and non-verbal responses to the photographs built up further understandings about the children's experiences and interests.

One of the children, for example had been engaged in a game of ball with his father. At the end of this play session the boy sees his father's boots and says 'Dad's boots'. The researchers take photographs during this activity and place them in an album. When the boy looks at the photographs of him playing with his father he is particularly interested in the photograph of the boots.

The different research tools, focusing on exploring children's perspectives helped to build up a composite picture of the experiences of parents and children.

Curriculum agendas

How does the Mosaic approach relate to current curriculum agendas? Throughout this report we have described this framework as being concerned with listening about living rather than listening about learning. However, these two processes of listening to children about their learning and listening about their experiences of being in an early childhood institution are interconnected. This can be seen to apply to the Early Years Foundation Stage where listening to young children can underpin each of the four themes: a unique child, positive relationships, enabling environments and learning and development (Hamer and Williams, 2010). This could draw attention to the value of listening to young children not as an extra activity when other priorities have been achieved but as an integral part of being learning communities.

Summary

In this report we have demonstrated the potential for using the Mosaic approach for listening to young children. We have shown how this work has built on others, drawing together advances in the use of participatory methods with children with early years pedagogy to form an approach which is multi-method, participatory, reflexive and adaptable. Our intention is that this study will be the starting point for others to build on these ideas in order to establish new ways of listening to young children.

Epilogue

Part 1 began by describing the Mosaic approach as an epistemological approach that seeks to provide opportunities for the construction and communication of knowledge. In subsequent studies by ourselves and others using and adapting the approach (for example, Stephenson, 2009) the importance of unhurried listening has been underlined:

> Participatory, visual research methods provide possibilities for young children and adults to engage in alternative forms of knowledge construction that in turn present challenges to researchers and research audiences. These complex explorations do not provide quick solutions to 'user engagement' but may contribute to new understandings between children and adults, professionals and lay communities. Perhaps this can be seen as a form of 'slow knowledge' not retrievable in the same way through a questionnaire but with the possibility of more rewarding and surprising results.
>
> (Clark, 2010b: 122)

This emphasis on the careful accumulation of knowledge, approaching research questions in an open-ended way does not sit well alongside tightly focused policy and practice agendas. However, such knowledge may produce new understandings on the views and experiences of both young children and adults, especially those most marginalised whose perspectives might be lost in a more rushed approach. Here listening can be seen to be linked to discussions of democratic education (for example Fielding and Moss, 2011).

The focus in this first study was on listening to young children. This was the primary research aim to develop methods to enable 'the voice of the child' to contribute to an evaluation of children's and family services. However, the question has arisen as to whether there is a need for specific methods which are seen as 'child-friendly' or whether within a participatory framework such methods may serve as 'participant-friendly' or person-friendly (Fraser, 2004)? The important factor here for us has been drawing together methods which 'play to the strengths' of the research participants. We have begun to use the Mosaic approach for researching with adults as well as young children (Clark, 2010a; Clark, 2011b).

The visual methods in particular have opened up opportunities for early childhood practitioners to step back and reflect on their own experiences of a specific environment. Visual narratives in the form of participant maps have provided a catalyst for dialogue within early childhood institutions and with other professionals from health, social welfare and architecture, with less day to day knowledge of early childhood practice. However the application of these research tools continue to require the careful consideration of ethical questions whether the participants are adults or young children. This need is heightened if research involves individuals from different professional backgrounds.

Time is required to make explicit taken-for-granted assumptions about childhood and research. Such exchanges are worth pursuing. The hope is that these struggles will result in new shared vocabularies, understandings and practices for more human ways of being.

Appendix

Further reading about the Mosaic approach

Listening to young children study

Clark, A 'The Mosaic Approach and research with young children' in Lewis, V, Kellett, M, Robinson, C, Fraser, S and Ding, S (eds) (2004) *The Reality of Research with Children and Young People.* London: Sage, 142–161.

This chapter is based on the first study using the Mosaic approach, as outlined in this book. The chapter is followed by a short personal commentary about the research process.

Spaces to Play study

Clark, A and Moss, P (2005) *Spaces to Play: more listening to young children using the Mosaic approach.* London: National Children's Bureau.

This second book about the Mosaic approach focuses on the adaptation of the approach to involve pre-school children in the redesign of their outdoor space. The book includes examples of how listening to children and adults using a range of visual and verbal methods led to practical changes to the preschool. The final part addresses questions for practitioners and researchers.

Clark, A 'Ways of seeing: using the Mosaic approach to listen to young children's perspectives' in Clark, A, Moss, P and Kjørholt, A (2005) *Beyond listening: children's perspectives on early childhood services.* Bristol: Policy Press, 29–49.

This chapter uses material from the Spaces to Play study to demonstrate how the Mosaic approach links with ideas about the pedagogy of listening, one of the cornerstones of practice in the pre-schools of Reggio Emilia as discussed by Carlina Rinaldi. Listening can involve self-reflection by children and adults as well as listening to others.

Living Spaces study

The Living Spaces study was a three year longitudinal project to investigate how young children and adults could be involved in the design and review of early childhood environments.

Clark, A (2008) Early childhood spaces: involving young children and practitioners in the design process. Working paper 45. The Hague: Bernard van Leer Foundation.

> This working paper gives a summary of the study, describing the two case studies: a new nursery class within a primary school and a review of a children's centre.

Clark, A (2010a) *Transforming children's spaces: children's and adults' participation in designing learning environments.* London: Routledge.

> This book is an account of the Mosaic approach in action in the context of learning communities who are undergoing change in their physical environment. The account describes the origins and adaption of the methods to focus on the design and review of spaces for children. One new development is a demonstration of how the Mosaic approach can aid reflection and communication by adults as well as children.

Clark, A (2010b) 'Young children as protagonists and the role of participatory, visual methods in engaging multiple perspectives', *American Journal of Community Psychology,* 46, 1–2, 115–123.

> This journal article explores the Mosaic approach within a participatory paradigm. Drawing on examples from three research studies, the article discusses how researching *with* young children rather than *on* young children can redraw the boundaries between adults' and children's roles in the research process including the relationship with the research audience.

Clark, A (2011a) 'Multimodal map making with young children: exploring ethnographic and participatory methods', *Qualitative Research* Special Issue *Multimodality and ethnography: working at the intersection* in Bella Dicks, Rosie Flewitt, Lesley Lancaster and Kate Pahl (eds) 11, 3, 311–330.

> This journal article focuses on the process of mapmaking within the Mosaic approach as a site of multi-modal communication. It investigates how the maps once completed can facilitate the exchange of meanings within learning communities and beyond.

Clark, A (2011b) 'Breaking methodological boundaries? Exploring visual, participatory methods with *adults* and young children' in Harcourt, D and Einarsdottir, J (eds) Children in research: (Special Issue: September). *European Early Childhood Research Journal*, 19(3) (Forthcoming).

This article explores the possibilities and challenges of extending the Mosaic approach as tools for listening to early childhood practitioners as well as to young children. The findings offer possibilities for re-examining rather than breaking the methodological boundaries in the field of early childhood between participatory research with young children and with adults.

References

Alderson, P (2000) *Young Children's Rights: exploring beliefs, principles and practice.* Jessica Kingsley/Save the Children.

Armstrong, J and Sugawara, A (1989) 'Children's perceptions of their day care experience', *Early Child Development and Care*, 49, 1–15.

Bartlett, K (1998) 'Real engagement by children', *Early Childhood Matters*, 9 (February 1999), 112–118.

Berghout Austin, A and others (1996) 'Determinants of children's satisfaction with their child care providers', *Early Child Development and Care*, 115, 19–36.

Bertram, T and Pascal, C (2008a) *Children Crossing Borders.* http://www.childrencrossingborders.org/index.html

Bertram, T and Pascal, C (2008b) *Opening Windows: A handbook for enhancing equity and diversity in early childhood settings.* Birmingham, UK: Amber Publications.

Calvert, S (2008) 'Children as Consumers: Advertising and Marketing', *The Future of Children*, 18, 1, 205–234.

Cattanach, A (1997) *Children's Stories in Play Therapy.* Jessica Kingsley.

Clark, A 'The Mosaic approach and research with young children' in Lewis, V, Kellett, M, Robinson, C, Fraser, S and Ding, S (eds) (2004) *The Reality of research with children and young people.* London: Sage.

Clark, A 'Ways of seeing: using the Mosaic approach to listen to young children's perspectives' in Clark, A, Moss, P and Kjørholt, A (2005) *Beyond listening: children's perspectives on early childhood services.* Bristol: Policy Press, 29–49.

Clark, A (2010a) *Transforming Children's Spaces: children's and adults' participation in designing learning environments.* London: Routledge.

Clark, A (2010b) 'Young children as protagonists and the role of participatory, visual methods in engaging multiple perspectives', *American Journal of Community Psychology*, 46, 1–2, 115–123.

Clark, A (2011a) 'Multimodal map making with young children: exploring ethnographic and participatory methods', *Qualitative Research* Special

Issue *Multimodality and ethnography: working at the intersection*, 11, 3, 311–330.

Clark, A (2011b) 'Breaking methodological boundaries? Exploring visual, participatory methods with adults and young children' in Harcourt, D and Einarsdottir, J (eds) Children in research: (Special Issue: September). *European Early Childhood Research Journal*, 19(3) (Forthcoming).

Clark, A and Moss, P (2005) *Spaces to Play: more listening to young children using the Mosaic approach*. London: National Children's Bureau.

Clark, A, Moss, P and Kjørholt, A (eds) (2005) *Beyond listening: children's perspectives on early childhood services*. Bristol: Policy Press.

Curtis, A 'Do we train our early educators to respect children?' in Nutbrown, C (ed) (1996) *Children's Rights and Early Education*. Paul Chapman Publishing.

Dahlberg, G, Moss, P and Pence, A (1999) *Beyond Quality in Early Childhood Education and Care: post modern perspectives*. Falmer Press.

Daycare Trust (1998) *Listening to Children. Young children's views on childcare: a guide for parents*. Daycare Trust.

Department of Education and Science (DES) (1991) *The Parent's Charter: you and your child's education*, revised 1994. DES.

Driscoll, V and Rudge, C (2005) 'Channels for listening to young children and parents' in Clark, A, Moss, P and Kjørholt, A *Beyond listening: children's perspectives on early childhood services*. Bristol: Policy Press, 91–110.

Early Childhood Education Forum (1998) *Quality and Diversity in Early Learning*. Early Childhood Education Forum and National Children's Bureau.

Edwards, C and others (1998) *The Hundred Languages of Children: the Reggio Emilia approach to early childhood education*, 2nd edn. New Jersey: Ablex Publishing Corporation.

Einarsdottir, J (2005) 'We can decide what to play! Children's perceptions of quality in an Icelandic playschool', *Early Education and Development*, 16, 4, 469–488.

Elfer, P and Selleck, D (1999) *The Best of Both Worlds: enhancing the experiences of young children in the nursery*. London: National Children's Bureau.

Evans, P and Fuller, M (1996) '"Hello, who am I speaking to?" Communicating with pre-school children in educational research settings', *Early Years*, 17, 1, 17–20.

Fielding, M and Moss, P (2011) *Radical Education and the Common School: a democratic alternative*. London: Routledge.

Fraser, S (2004) 'Situating Empirical Research' in Fraser, S, Lewis, V, Ding, S, Kellett, M and Robinson, C (eds) Doing Research with Children and Young People. London: Sage, 15–26.

Goldschmied, E and Jackson, S (1994) *People Under Three: young children in daycare*. London: Routledge.

Hamer, C and Williams, L (2010) *Let's Listen*. London: National Children's Bureau.

Hart, R (1997) *Children's Participation*. UNICEF and Earthscan.

Hennessy, E (1999) 'Children as Service Evaluators', *Child Psychology and Psychiatry*, 4, 4, 153–160.

Hodges, J and Steele, M (2000) Effects of abuse on attachment representations: Narrative assessment of abused children. *Journal of Child Psychotherapy*, 26(3), 433–455.

James, A and Prout, A (1997) *Constructing and Reconstructing Childhood*, 2nd edn. Falmer Press.

Johnson, V and Ivan-Smith, E (1995) *Listening to smaller voices*. Actionaid.

Johnson, V and others (eds) (1998) *Stepping Forward. Children and young people's participation in the development process*. Intermediate Technology.

Joseph, S (ed) (1999) *A Voice for the Child: the inspirational words of Janusz Korczak*. Thorsons.

Lancaster, YP and Kirby, P on behalf of Coram (2010) *Listening to young children*, 2nd edn. Buckingham: Open University Press.

Langsted, O 'Looking at quality from the child's perspective' in Moss, P and Pence, A (eds) (1994) *Valuing Quality in Early Childhood Services: new approaches to defining quality*. Paul Chapman Publishing.

Lee, N (2001) *Childhood and Society: growing up in an age of uncertainty*. Buckingham: Open University Press.

Marchant, R (1999) *Listening on all Channels*. Triangle Services.

Mayall, B (1996) *Children, Health and Social Order*. Open University Press.

McNeish, D (1999) *From Rhetoric to Reality: participatory approaches to health promotion with young people*. Health Education Authority.

Miller, J (1997) *Never too young: how young children can take responsibility and make decisions*. London: National Early Years Network.

Nutbrown, C (ed) (1996) *Children's Rights and Early Education*. Paul Chapman Publishing.

Oakley, A (2000) *Experiments in Knowing: Gender and Method in the Social Sciences*. New York: New Press.

O'Kane, C 'The development of participatory techniques: facilitating children's views about decisions which affect them' in Christensen, P and James, A (eds) (2000) *Research with Children: perspectives and practice.* Falmer Press.

Paige-Smith, A and Rix, J (2011) 'Researching early intervention and young children's perspectives – developing and using a "listening to children approach"', *British Journal of Special Education*, 38, 1, 28–36.

Paley, V (1981) *Wally's Stories.* London: Harvard University Press.

Paley, V (1986) 'On listening to what children have to say', *Harvard Educational Review*, 56, 2, 122–131.

Paley, V (1997) *The Girl with the Brown Crayon.* London: Harvard University Press.

Pascal, C and Bertram, T (eds) (1997) *Effective Early Learning: case studies in improvement.* Hodder.

Pascal, C and Bertram,T (2009) 'Listening to young citizens: the struggle to make real a participatory paradigm in research with young children', *European Early Childhood Education Research Journal*, 17, 2, June, 249–262.

Prosser, J (2007) 'Visual methods and the visual culture of schools', *Visual studies*, 22, 1, 13–30.

Prosser, J and Loxley, A (2008) Introducing Visual Methods. National Centre for Research Methods Review Papers. NCRM/010. Unpublished.

Prout, A. (2005) *The Future of Childhood.* London: RoutledgeFalmer.

Pugh, G and Selleck, D 'Listening to and communicating with young children' in Davie, R and others (1996) *The Voice of the Child: a handbook for professionals.* Falmer Press.

Qvortrup, J (1987) 'Introduction: the sociology of childhood', *International Journal of Sociology*, 17 (3) 3–37.

Ribbens, J and Edwards, R (eds) (1998) *Feminist dilemmas in qualitative research: public knowledge and private lives.* London: Sage.

Richardson, L and Adams St. Pierre, E (2008) Writing: a method of inquiry in Denzin, N and Lincoln, Y (eds) Collecting and Interpreting Qualitative Materials. 3rd edition. Thousand Oaks, California: Sage, 473–500.

Rinaldi, C (2006) *In dialogue with Reggio Emilia: listening, researching and learning.* London: Routledge.

Steele, M and others (1999) 'The use of story stem narratives in assessing the inner world of the child: implications for adoptive placements' in Assessment, Preparation and Support: implications from research. London: British Agency for Adoption and Fostering.

Stephenson, A (2009) 'Horses in the sandpit: photography, prolonged involvement and "stepping back" as strategies for listening to children's voices', *Early Child Development & Care*, 179, 2, 131–141.

Tangen, R (2008) 'Listening to children's voices in educational research: some theoretical and methodological problems', *European Journal of Special Needs Education*, 23, 2, May, 157–166.

Thomson, P (ed) (2008) *Doing visual research with children and young people*. London: Routledge.

Tolfree, D (1996) Restoring playfulness. Stockhom, Sweden: Rädda Barnen.

Tolfree, D and Woodhead, M (1999) 'Tapping a key resource', Early Childhood Matters, 91, (February), 19–23.

Veale, A 'Creative methodologies in participatory research with children' in Greene, S and Hogan, D (eds) (2005) *Researching Children's Experience: approaches and methods. London: Sage.

Vecchi, V (2009) *Art and creativity in Reggio Emilia: exploring the role and potential of ateliers in early childhood education*. London: Routledge.

Walker, R (1993) 'Finding a silent voice for the researcher: using photographs in evaluation and research' in Schratz, M (ed) Qualitative Voices in Educational Research: London: Falmer Press.

Wigfall, V and Moss, P (2001) *More than the sum of its parts? A study of a multi-agency childcare network*. London: National Children's Bureau for the Joseph Rowntree Foundation.

Index